HOW TO ASSESS

MORTGAGES & LOANS

Designed and produced by Templar Publishing Ltd
107 High Street, Dorking, Surrey RH4 1QA
Typeset by Templar Type
Printed and bound in Great Britain
by Richard Clay Ltd
Chichester, Sussex

British Library Cataloguing in Publication Data

Cawthorne, Nigel
How to assess mortgages and loans.—
(You and your money series)
1. Finance, Personal—Great Britain
—Handbooks, manuals, etc.
I. Title   II. Series
332.024'00941   HG179

ISBN 0-7063-6647-6

HOW TO ASSESS

MORTGAGES & LOANS

NIGEL CAWTHORNE

Ward Lock · London

CONTENTS

INTRODUCTION

The UK housing market has been characterised for many years by steady growth in owner-occupation. The laws of supply and demand, coupled with inflation and an accompanying rise in the value of real assets, have created buoyant trading conditions, especially since about 1950. Because the overwhelming majority of homes are acquired with the aid of a house purchase loan – or mortgage – the lenders have been doing well too.

At the beginning of this century, over 90 per cent of the population of the UK lived in rented or shared accommodation. As recently as the Second World War only about 25 per cent of homes were owned by their occupants. The demand for housing, caused by the steady growth in population among other factors, was largely met by local authorities. Council houses plus the accommodation offered by private landlords, meant that about 65 per cent of all households were still in rented accommodation in the mid-1950s.

Partly as a result of revelations of scandalous exploitation by private landlords, a succession of Rent Acts were passed which strengthened tenants' rights and curbed some of the excesses of landlords who, with little incentive to maintain properties at their own expense, had passed much of the burden on to oppressed tenants. In particular, the Rent Act of 1956 put tenants in such a strong position that, as many of them complained, it was the landlords that became the oppressed species.

Privately rented accommodation soon became scarce, and that, plus the inadequacy of council housing, prompted a growing number of householders to think in terms of owner-occupation. There were positive pressures in the same direction. Significant tax concessions were offered to encourage owner-occupation, and government policy has generally continued to favour it, especially in the 1980s. The psychological aspect should not be neglected either. In England, 'the Englishman's home is his castle' and owner-occupation has become an almost universal aspiration. Consequently, the proportion of households in owner-occupation has more than doubled since 1950.

Despite the rising price of houses, mortgage hunting today is not the nightmare business it was a few years ago. The mortgage market now consists of over 200 different lenders, including building societies, banks, insurance companies, finance houses, even specialist mortgage corporations, created only to lend and not to provide any other service. This vast and still growing choice has, however, created its own problems. All these institutions lend money on their own lending terms, and it is surprising what large differences exist between them. For example, a couple earning £10,000 were recently offered a loan of £35,000 by one institution and £60,000 by another!

Interest rates also vary. The rate can differ by as much as 2 per cent, and the different methods used to calculate the interest may stretch the difference by another percentage point.

The would-be borrower has a great many choices to make, and at first he or she is likely to be bewildered by the sheer range of alternatives. Besides the interest rates, he must consider the method of repayment. The borrower is probably aware that more than one kind of mortgage is available and that repayment differs between straight repayment mortgages and endowment mortgages. But does he know that there is more than one type of repayment mortgage?

And then, what about pension mortgages? Are they more suitable since the change in the law that came into effect in 1988? If this type of mortgage looks promising, should the borrower use a personal plan or executive plan? Should he stay in a group scheme, or set up a self-adminstered fund?

The mortgage market is by no means the jungle it may appear, but it is important to arrange a mortgage or other loan that suits your particular requirements. Don't settle for the first option available. A number of innovative schemes have recently appeared on the market. They are worth examining, but remember that the obvious advantages they may offer are probably balanced by less obvious snags. Different schemes provide for fixed rates, low-interest payments in the early years, interest-only loans, constant payments irrespective of rate changes and insurance against untoward rises in cost. Which of these, if any, is of interest to you?

Such choices are not limited to those buying a home. Existing borrowers may benefit from examining their current arrangements in the light of these market changes, especially if they have acquired new commitments in the form of bank loans, a second home, school fees, etc.

A mortgage should not be treated in isolation from total personal finance and long-term plans. It represents both your largest debt and your greatest asset and it is, therefore, worth seeking the best impartial advice before you embark on it.

PART I

MORTGAGES

WHAT IS A MORTGAGE?

A mortgage is a long term loan for buying property, with the property itself standing as security for the loan. This means that if you fail to pay back the loan, the lender – usually a building society or a bank – can compel you to sell the property and repay them out of the proceeds. In legal language, the lender has first charge on the property. Although the deeds are in your name and you have title to the property, there are restrictions on what you can do with it until you have cleared the loan.

HOW IS IT PAID BACK?

Mortgages usually run for 20 or 25 years; a longer period is sometimes allowed, depending on the earning prospects of the borrower. There are several methods of repaying the loan. You can make monthly instalments which re-pay the original loan plus interest over the agreed period. Alternatively, you can take an interest-only mortgage, in which you pay only the interest on the loan in monthly instalments to the lender, the loan itself being repaid through a life-assurance policy, pension or similar device.

WHO WILL PROVIDE ONE?

Traditionally, mortgages on homes have been provided almost exclusively by building societies. These were institutions established during the last century to lend their members the money to buy their own home at favourable rates. Local small investors clubbed together to save money, so that each could eventually buy their own home.

The building societies have continued this benevolent, non-profit-making role. Building society investors and borrowers are still 'members' rather than customers. The societies, despite their immense wealth and financial power, make no profit. The small margin between the interest rate paid to investors and the rate charged to borrowers merely covers administration costs.

The largest societies now have hundreds of branches throughout the country and assets that run into billions. Fierce competition for business between the building societies in the UK has led them to brush up their image. Their TV advertising for example emphasises their friendly service. Though they are no longer permitted to act as a cartel, co-operation between the societies is close and there is little variation between them in terms of interest rates. This smiling face has killed the old image of the reluctant lender. Building societies today are enthusiastic lenders, even to those who have not invested with them.

But the building societies are no longer unchallenged in the domestic mortgage business. High street banks have moved in to the lucrative mortgage market, followed by foreign and merchant banks, and even insurance companies. All of these see the mortgage and property market as a safe investment – as safe as houses!

WHY DO YOU WANT TO BORROW?

Most people in the UK want to own their own home but most of them cannot afford it unless they borrow the purchase price by taking out a mortgage. Rented accommodation is in any case difficult to find. The major landlords are local councils who impose serious limits on their tenants. They often make it difficult to move, prevent changes or improvements to the property and may impose other restrictions, such as a ban on pets. In a home you own, you can do more or less as you like.

For most people the financial advantages of home ownership are compelling. Money paid in rent could equally well go towards mortgage repayments. Moreover, buying a property with a mortgage provides not only a home but also a valuable asset. At the end of the mortgage term, the house is yours and you have no more to pay – except for the rates and maintenance, of course. And, as house prices rise, you can sell your house at any time during the term of the mortgage, re-pay the mortgage company, and take your profit.

WHY DO MORTGAGE COMPANIES WANT TO LEND MONEY?

Building societies, banks and insurance companies have a great deal of capital, which they must invest. Some institutions invest in stocks and shares, others invest directly in businesses or grant loans on which they charge interest. The return on much of this investment is high, but some of it is risky. Share prices may fall, businesses may go bankrupt, loans may not be repaid. Large financial institutions are therefore always on the look-out for a safe investment that will give them a steady return over a long period.

Like the individual house buyer, mortgage companies recognise that one of the safest investments available is the British housing market. Demand is always growing and prices tend to rise constantly. When they lend money to a house purchaser, they can feel reasonably confident. Normally, the loan is repaid regularly at a steady rate of interest. If the borrower defaults, they can regain their money by compelling the sale of the house. If the borrower dies, the mortgage is usually covered by a life policy. They can't go wrong.

For the building societies the situation is not as cold-blooded as that. They were founded as non-profit-making institutions with the sole aim of helping people buy houses. When you borrow from them you become a member of that society and they are committed to helping you out.

The high street banks, foreign banks, merchant banks and insurance companies have all entered the market because it is the safest investment around. In fact, from the lender's point of view, it is so safe that the new mortgage-only companies may actually sell off individual mortgages to other financial institutions to keep themselves in cash. A mortgage may change hands several times during its lifetime.

HOW MORTGAGES ARE SECURED

The principle of the mortgage depends upon the property. Without a house, there is no loan (and, often, without a loan there is no house!). But there are all sorts of houses on the market. Some are regarded less favourably than others.

New houses are favoured by most lenders. If built by a reputable builder the lender can be reasonably confident that the house has no major structural faults and will retain or increase its value over the life of the mortgage. Many building societies co-operate with reputable builders to arrange mortgages directly while the purchase is being made.

Council houses sold at a discount to sitting tenants are also attractive to lenders, as the value of the property exceeds the amount they are asked to lend. Again mortgage companies often co-operate directly with councils to supply mortgages to tenants who are buying under the government's 'Right to Buy' scheme.

VALUATION

Because the value of a house is the mortgage company's only protection if the borrower fails to repay the loan, it is careful to ensure that the value of the property exceeds or, at worst, equals the value of the loan and that it is not likely to decline. Most companies make their own valuation; they often insist that the borrower puts up some of the money. Their valuation is normally a little lower than the market price because it is supposed to represent the price that the house could be sold for if the mortgage company has to sell it quickly. And the sum lent is usually less than the company's valuation in order to leave a margin for safety. Yet even if everything does go wrong and the company eventually forces the sale of the house at a price lower than the sum they have lent, it is the borrower who stands the loss – just as he takes the profit if the selling price is higher than the price he paid.

DIFFICULT PROPERTIES

Naturally there are some categories of housing which are less attractive to potential lenders. There are broad guidelines on this type of property. For example, you are unlikely to be offered a mortgage if the house you want to buy is: on the edge of a cliff; on the point of collapse; in very poor condition; subject to a demolition order or likely to become so (a frequent problem with inner-city properties); on a lease which will run for less than about 25 years after the mortgage ends.

Mortgage companies also look warily at older properties. They are cautious about houses built before 1920, even more of houses built before 1900. But it should not be too difficult to raise a mortgage on an older property if it is in good repair.

Lenders favour houses that can be resold quickly, but tend to be reluctant about houses without gardens. They are less keen on converted flats or maisonettes unless they are in urban areas and the conversion has been done to a reasonable standard. Properties with sitting tenants also present difficulties. Companies avoid lending on the freehold – rather than the leasehold – of flats and maisonettes because of the likely controversies over who pays for the repair and maintenance of the building.

Lenders may turn down a mortgage application for a property without basic amenities like a lavatory or bathroom, or they may withhold part of the mortgage until appropriate alterations have been made. On a seriously dilapidated house, they may offer a proportion of the valuation or withhold part of the loan pending specified repairs, or they may specify that such repairs are made within a certain period, perhaps six months.

THE LEGAL SIDE OF MORTGAGES

Normally, when you buy a house with the help of a building society, bank or insurance company, your solicitor will send you a mortgage deed for you to sign and should also explain broadly what it is all about. But, as you are responsible for the mortgage and it is your signature on the deed, it is best that you understand the various legal terms it contains.

MORTGAGE, PLEDGE AND CHARGE

There are several types of secured loans. The term 'pledge' is well known in connection with pawnshops: the pawnbroker lends you money on the security of some valuable object that you deposit at his shop. The pawnbroker, or pledgee, gets possession of the object but not ownership. That remains with the customer, or pledgor. With a true mortgage the situation is reversed. The lender's interest in the property gives ownership, while the borrower retains possession.

However, most mortgages are not of this type. Most involve the principle of a *charge*. This gives the lender, or chargee, no interest in the property, only certain rights over it. It is probably a charge that you are giving when you sign the mortgage deed.

MORTGAGOR AND MORTGAGEE

The borrower of the money is called the mortgagor and the lender – the mortgage company – is called the mortgagee. The capital sum borrowed is called the mortgage debt. This is different from other types of debt because it is secured against a property. If the mortgagor does not pay the mortgage debt back, the mortgagee has the power to force the sale of the mortgaged property and reclaim the debt from the proceeds.

SUCCESSIVE MORTGAGES

You can have more than one mortgage. In fact, there is no limit to the number of mortgages you can have on your property (though in practice it would be difficult to find anyone to lend you more money once the mortgages you have already taken exceed the value of the property). If you default, the mortgagees take their money in order of date, i.e. the earliest first. That is why second and subsequent lenders charge more. They take a bigger risk because the first mortgagee has precedence in the event of a default.

THE RIGHTS OF THE MORTGAGOR

The mortgagor has the right to redeem the mortgage, so there must be no restrictions on his ability to re-pay the mortgage. The mortgagee cannot create a mortgage that is impossible to redeem, and there must be no condition which binds the mortgagor to the lender after they have re-paid the mortgage. A mortgage cannot be converted into another type of loan. In the eyes of the law, once a mortgage always a mortgage.

THE RIGHTS OF THE MORTGAGEE

In some cases, the mortgagee has the legal right to take possession of the property if you default. But this rarely happens. If the mortgage is by deed, the mortgagee has the power of sale. This arises only after you have failed to pay, and is only exercised under strict conditions. If you default, the mortgagee often has the right to put in a receiver to collect any rents or profits that you might be getting from the property. The mortgagee can take the equity in the property by means of foreclosure. But building societies and other lenders only take this step as a last resort. If you fall on hard times through illness, unemployment, etc., the lender will often help by adjusting the repayments, perhaps by claiming interest only for a limited period. Mortgage companies want their money, not your house.

TYPES OF MORTGAGES

A mortgage is a loan. When you take out a loan, you must repay not only the sum borrowed, but also interest on that sum. The interest may be fixed throughout the term of the loan or for a specified period. More often, the rate is variable, and roughly follows changes in bank interest rates. Although the exact rate can vary, the principle is the same for all types of mortgages. But there are several ways to repay the capital sum, and it is the method of doing this which accounts for the main differences between different types of mortgage.

REPAYMENT MORTGAGES

The simplest way to re-pay a mortgage is to pay each month's interest together with a small amount of the capital. There are two types of repayment mortgage: the old-fashioned gross profile (or rising net repayment mortgage) and the annuity (or constant net repayment mortgage) which is now much more common.

In a gross profile mortgage, the interest payments and capital repayments are worked out over the whole term of the mortgage so that you pay roughly the same each month throughout the life of the mortgage. Your precise repayment is usually calculated on an annual basis (say, in January) which takes interest rate changes into account, so your monthly repayments do not change during that year even if interest rates do. In some cases though, variations in interest rates are taken into account month by month.

With this type of mortgage, you pay mainly interest at the start making only the tiniest repayments on the capital. As time goes on, the amount of capital you owe decreases and, as you owe less, you have less interest to pay. Your monthly payment therefore includes a rising proportion of the capital.

Because you receive tax relief on the interest (but not on the capital repayment), with a gross profile or rising net repayment mortgage, benefit from tax relief is greater at the beginning of the mortgage and less at the end. So, while the gross repayment stays the same, what you actually pay each month rises throughout the term of the mortgage. The extra tax relief at the beginning makes this type of mortgage a suitable 'easy-start' loan for many homeowners.

However, much more common today is the annuity or constant net repayment mortgage. Building societies often offer only this type, and heavy persuasion is necessary if you want another type of mortgage.

The term constant repayment means that monthly repayments are calculated to remain roughly constant throughout the term of the mortgage *after* tax relief is taken into account. With constant net repayment mortgages, monthly repayments vary according to prevailing rates. However, you pay less overall with a constant net repayment mortgage because you pay off the capital sum more quickly and thus pay less interest in the long term. Different types of repayment mortgage suit different people, depending on personal income, income tax status and the price of the property.

ENDOWMENT MORTGAGES

An endowment mortgage is essentially two things: a simple loan – the money you need to buy the house – and an endowment policy from an insurance company. Repayments to the mortgage company consist of interest on the loan exclusively, and tax relief on repayments remains the same throughout the life of the mortgage (disregarding changes in interest rates). At the end of the term, the capital – the original loan – must be repaid. The endowment policy is designed to accomplish this.

REPAYMENT MORTGAGE v INTEREST ONLY MORTGAGE

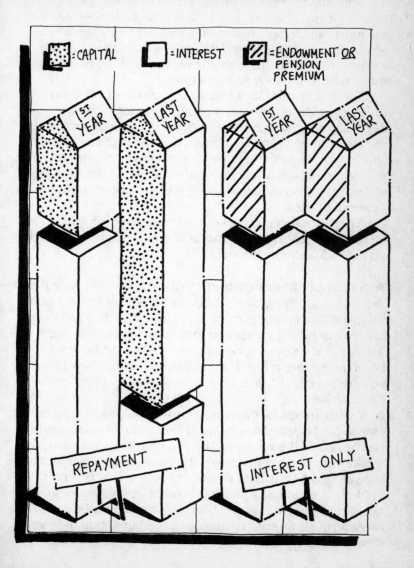

With an endowment mortgage, an endowment policy from an insurance company is taken out at the same time as the mortgage. It has the same term as the mortgage and its terminal value is calculated to be the same amount as the loan. At the end of the term, the proceeds of the policy are made over to the mortgage company.

There may even be a bonus. Some forms of endowment policy provide a surplus at the end of the term, its size depending on the performance of the insurance company in the intervening years. This surplus can be taken as a lump sum, so you can actually make money on your mortgage! The policy also provides life cover, so that if you die the mortgage is paid off immediately, relieving your bereaved family of a financial burden.

There are several types of endowment policy which can be used to repay a mortgage loan. The most suitable depends on individual circumstances.

● **A non-profit endowment policy** repays the capital at the end of the mortgage but carries no bonus. It is not good value for money as it is more expensive than a conventional repayment mortgage with no long-term advantages. Many 'top-up' and second mortgages are of this type, however, because they are offered by insurance companies which require purchase of a non-profit endowment policy to pay back the loan.

● **A with-profit endowment policy** provides both the cash to pay back the capital and, if the insurance company has performed well, a substantial bonus. Only the amount of the capital sum is guaranteed, and the eventual profits might be outweighed by the extra cost of the policy. That is very unlikely, but a with-profits endowment mortgage does work out fairly expensive in the short term and it may be worth considering how much could be earned investing the extra cost of the premiums elsewhere.

● **Low-cost endowment mortgages** have become the most popular way of repaying a mortgage. The endowment policy in this case is for a lower basic sum than the mortgage but, as it is a with-profits policy, the amount payable at the end should be sufficient to repay the loan when the bonuses and profits are added. Although there can be no guarantee that the proceeds from the policy will cover the debt at maturity, insurance companies use only a proportion of the anticipated bonuses in their calculations (usually, about 80 per cent of reversionary bonuses and excluding any terminal bonus). It is therefore reasonable to expect there to be a cash surplus over and above the funds required to repay the mortgage loan.

This type of policy also provides life cover for the full amount of the mortgage. It is the cheapest form of endowment mortgage and compares well with the cost of an ordinary repayment mortgage.

● **The low-start, low-cost endowment mortgage** is a variation which permits lower premiums at the start. Premiums increase slowly over the first five or ten years and level off at a slightly higher rate than those of a straight low-cost mortgage.

This is an attractive option to people who can expect their income to rise fast enough to keep up with the increased payments. By saving on the mortgage repayments during the first few years of occupation money becomes available for improvements. On the other hand, for those who have not yet started a family and in the meantime perhaps enjoy two incomes, this is probably not a suitable type of mortgage.

UNIT-LINKED 'ENDOWMENT' MORTGAGE

Another way to accumulate the capital to pay back the original loan is by investing in unit-linked funds. There is a higher risk involved here, as investments can go down as as well as up. An interest-only mortgage loan is taken out, but this time it is linked to a unit plan. Monthly payments to this plan are invested in units allocated to different funds or investment portfolios.

If the underlying investments perform well, the rewards can be far greater than under an endowment policy. If they perform badly, monthly payments may be increased. However, the mortgagee does not want to risk a default on the loan at the end of the term and therefore reviews the situation ten years before and again five years before the end of the term. Early warning of possible difficulties is then available.

PENSION-LINKED MORTGAGES

Endowment policies are not the only way to build up sufficient capital to re-pay the mortgage company's loan on your house. Theoretically, any method will do, provided the lender feels sufficiently confident of getting the money back in the end.

Pension-linked mortgages offer one alternative, and they are growing in popularity. Once again, an interest-only mortgage loan is taken out. A pension plan is taken out with an insurance company to provide a monthly income after retirement plus a lump sum sufficient to pay back the purchase price of your house at the end of the term.

The current popularity of this method is due to the tax relief situation. While tax relief on insurance premiums has been withdrawn, it is allowed on pension plan payments. This makes a pension-linked mortgage one of the most tax-efficient ways of buying a home, especially for a high earner.

Obviously, there is also the advantage of arranging a pension at the same time as the mortgage, of particular interest to someone who is self-employed or in a job without a pension. But this type of mortgage is now open to all, and members of occupational pension schemes can also benefit. It is possible to arrange a pension-linked mortgage by using any retirement lump sum to pay back the capital at the end of the mortgage term.

FIXED RATE MORTGAGES

With most mortgages the interest rate you pay fluctuates as banks and building societies change their interest rates, but it is possible to take out a mortgage with fixed interest at a rate which is usually lower than the market average, for an agreed period. You may find yourself paying up to 1 per cent below the market rate for up to twelve months or longer. However, if interest rates drop, you will be paying more than the market rate.

INTEREST-ONLY MORTGAGES

Some borrowers prefer to make their own provision for the repayment of a mortgage debt. Older borrowers may be limited by the number of years of repayments they would be granted by a lender. Some borrowers only require short term facilities. For people in these categories an interest-only mortgage may be suitable.

Interest-only loans are available for five years onward. They do not require the assignment of an endowment policy, nor are any capital repayments necessary during the term. The debt is normally repaid from the sale of the property or other assets.

The chief advantage of an interest-only mortgage is that the borrower is free to take advantage of other investment opportunities, such as personal equity plans. Through such means he can amass a lump sum for eventual repayment of the mortgage.

An older borrower is normally restricted by the shorter time before retirement age in which to repay a mortgage. With an interest-only loan over a short period of time, monthly repayments are kept to a minimum. The loan is repaid on retirement from the realisation of other assets such as pension funds, or by sale of the property. (When people retire, they often move into a smaller and cheaper house, which results in surplus cash to re-pay the mortgage.)

This type of mortgage also suits foreigners resident in the UK for a short time. They may wish to purchase a property rather than rent one to take advantage of what has traditionally been a buoyant British property market. But making capital repayments would be somewhat impractical as they would have little impact on the outstanding debt yet would represent a significant amount of the monthly repayments. If the debt is repaid from the sale of the property when the owner leaves the country, the value of the property has probably gone up, leaving a cash profit.

ROLL-UP INTEREST MORTGAGE

In this comparatively new scheme, the well-to-do borrower does not even have to pay the whole of the interest. Say he has a house worth £200,000 and wants a mortgage of £140,000. The lender charges interest on £40,000 as a monthly repayment but the interest on the 100,000 becomes 'roll-up' which means it is added to the loan. Instead of the capital sum borrowed decreasing during the term of the mortgage, it actually increases. But if house prices climb faster, the borrower still makes a profit. Again, the lender is repaid when the property is sold or by the sale of other assets.

This type of mortgage is only available to those whom the lender considers a very good risk. It is an attractive proposition especially to people in the financial world because they can live in a house that is much more expensive than they could otherwise afford while using the money they save in more profitable investments. When they retire, they can sell up, take what profit there is and possibly move into a smaller house in the country, where prices are lower.

FUTURE DEVELOPMENTS

Mortgage lenders are constantly devising new schemes and in future there may be many other types of mortgage. One that is already common in the United States but has not yet reached Britain is the transferable mortgage.

This type of mortgage belongs to the property, not to the owner. When the owner sells the house he sells the mortgage along with it, and the buyer takes up the mortgage repayments and pays for the equity in the property – that is, the difference between the market price and the amount outstanding on the mortgage. To do this, he may have to raise a second mortgage on the property.

With this arrangement, the market value of the property is not just the intrinsic value of the house itself, it reflects the condition of the mortgage too. If the mortgage is particularly favourable it increases the price the vendor can charge for the property.

These are the main types of mortgage, available today. You may hear other names applied to mortgages, like 'LIBOR-linked', 'low-start' and 'cap and collar', but these terms apply only to the way the interest is paid, not to the type of mortgage.

THE LENDERS

The British property market is at present so attractive that financial institutions from all over the world are attempting to move into it. Building societies which once lent exclusively to members now offer non-members mortgages and even personal loans. Banks which were formerly content to make their money out of businesses and overdrafts now encourage customers to take out a mortgage with them. Merchant banks accustomed to financing major projects and foreign banks who were once content with purely domestic enterprises are hustling for mortgage business through brokers. Mortgage-only companies have sprung up and 'trade' mortgages like other investments.

BUILDING SOCIETIES

Although building societies, no longer have the field to themselves, they still account for about 50 per cent of current home loans. There are some 130 building societies in Britain, most of which are members of the Building Societies Association. This association was in effect a cartel, the members of which fixed the mortgage rate. These days it is merely a trade association; the building societies fix their interest rates without collusion, though naturally they tend to rise and fall at roughly the same time and, by roughly the same amount, following the banks' minimum lending rate.

The societies do still give preference to people who have savings accounts with them, but when capital is abundant they are naturally less discriminating in their loans policy.

If you are planning to take a mortgage with a building society it is advisable to save with more than one, so you have a choice when the time comes. Before you open an account ask for a leaflet summarising the mortgage terms. It is pointless to save with a society which, for example, won't lend on a conversion if you are looking for a flat in an area where there are few purpose-built blocks! Ask about their other financial services such as personal loans and credit cards, which you may need in the future. As for your savings acccount, a regular monthly saving plan will earn you extra interest.

BANKS

The big four high street banks – Barclays, National Westminster, Lloyds and Midland – all offer home loans. So do other banks, such as the Clydesdale, the Co-operative, the Royal Bank of Scotland, the Bank of Scotland and the Trustee Savings Bank.

Your bank, of course, knows your financial situation as well as anyone. It sees how much money comes in and how much goes out. It can therefore easily assess how reliable you are. There is also an advantage for you in having all your finances handled by a single organisation.

Bank interest rates tend to be slightly higher than building societies and they charge an arrangement fee – usually about £100. But because of the way banks calculate interest, your monthly payments may work out about the same.

Foreign banks don't have the cost of running branches all over this country, and they can offer a centralised, streamlined service. Banks like the Bank of Ireland or the (American) Chemical Bank sometimes offer good terms on large loans or to buyers making a large deposit. Mortgages with other foreign banks can be arranged through brokers.

INSURANCE COMPANIES

About twenty insurance companies have mortgage funds to lend at interest rates competitive with, and sometimes even cheaper than, those from building societies and banks. They are, naturally, endowment mortgages. Most operate through mortgage and insurance brokers, although some – such as

Abbey Life Home Loans and Prudential Home Loans – are now marketing their products direct. Insurance companies are also a ready source of top-up loans if your first mortgage offer is too small for your needs.

BROKERS

The mortgage market can be a bewildering place and a mortgage and insurance broker is a ready source of advice. The broker is not actually the source of finance but he can arrange a mortgage for you from one of the many banks, building societies and insurance companies, and if you have a particular problem, the broker will know where best to place your application.

Brokers often offer innovative mortgage packages which can be tailored to fit your needs. As mortgage lenders become more sophisticated, it is becoming common for particularly favourable mortgages to be offered for a brief period, perhaps a month or two. The ordinary borrower can hardly keep up with such developments without a broker's help.

All reputable brokers are members of FIMBRA (the *Financial Intermediaries, Managers and Brokers Regulatory Association*), the industry's regulatory organisation, which aims to ensure that brokers give the best independent advice to their clients.

BUILDERS

Large property developers and builders, especially those developing estates of new houses, often have financial arrangements with building societies. They will arrange a mortgage and sometimes offer low rates for the first year as an incentive.

LOCAL AUTHORITIES

Mortgages are often arranged by local councils for purchasers of council houses under the Right to Buy scheme. Councils will also offer mortgages on cheaper or older – pre-Second World War – housing. They may well offer a mortgage on a property on which the building societies have refused loans. But their funds are limited, as the government restricts the amount they can lend. Still, if you cannot obtain a mortgage anywhere else, an approach to the local council is well worthwhile.

EMPLOYERS

Employees of banks, insurance companies and building societies are sometimes offered low-interest mortgages. Many large companies with links to building societies and insurance companies arrange mortgages for their employees on favourable terms. A snag can arise if the employee leaves the company, and thereupon has to pay the full rate.

MORTGAGE COMPANIES

Recently a number of mortgage-only companies have sprung up. As they deal only with mortgages they tend to be quick and efficient. However, speed and efficiency depend on the free running of all parts, and any unusual feature or financial difficulty can dislocate the process. Production-line mortgages may not be suitable for people who anticipate financial problems.

HOW MUCH CAN I BORROW?

The amount you can borrow depends on your income, the amount of mortgage funds on the market and the value of the property you want to buy. But that does not mean that all mortgage companies will offer to lend you the same amount on the same property. The way they work out how much they are willing to lend you varies considerably even from one building society to another. If your first offer is unsatisfactory, it is well worth investigating others.

THE INCOME EQUATION
Building societies and banks usually offer a sum between two-and-a-half and three times your annual income, plus between one and one-and-a-half times any additional incomes if the house is being bought by more than one person. The most common example of the latter is a house bought jointly by a husband and wife, but most mortgage companies will accept two single people as joint owners. Three or more joint owners may encounter resistance.

Even married couples will find that the way in which mortgage companies work out the figures on the two incomes varies considerably. In an extreme case, they may add the two incomes together and multiply them by one-and-a-half or two or more.

Some lenders will take regular overtime or spare-time earnings into account. If the applicant is self-employed, some will take an accountant's word for his or her income, while others will demand three years' accounts.

Advertisements for so-called 'non-status' mortgages (where the lender asks for no proof of income) usually omit to mention that the interest you pay will be loaded and the amount lent will be a smaller percentage of the value of the home.

HOW MUCH CAN I BORROW ?

Income	3 X INCOME	2½ X INCOME	1½ X INCOME
£1,000 P.A.	3,000	2,500	1,500
£2,500 P.A.	7,500	6,250	3,750
£5,000 P.A.	15,000	12,500	7,500
£10,000 P.A.	30,000	25,000	15,000
£15,000 P.A.	45,000	37,500	22,500
£25,000 P.A.	75,000	62,500	37,500

THE STATE OF THE MARKET

If the market is tight, naturally mortgages are less easily obtained. Lenders may offer much less than expected. Similarly, if money is plentiful, companies may improve their offers and be more willing to overlook problems. Sometimes it pays to wait – if you can. The danger is that, by taking advantage of the easy money market, you may find yourself in difficulty later – if, for instance, interest rates rise, you lose your job, or your mortgage partner stops working.

THE PROPERTY

Lenders make their own valuation of the property. This is likely to be slightly lower than the true market value as the lender will assess the price to be expected on a quick sale in the event of the borrower defaulting on mortgage payments. The lender's valuation may bear little relation to what the individual is prepared to pay for the property. The lender will then be prepared to advance a proportion of this figure. For example, you may be offering to pay £25,000 for a house, which the lender values at £24,000. The lender, whether bank, insurance company or building society, may have a lending limit of 80 to 95 per cent of the valuation. So the sum you are offered may be only £21,500. If the property is older – for example, a terraced house built in the 1920s – the lender's limit may be 75 per cent of the valuation.

You may be offered a 100 per cent mortgage on a new house – by the builder, say, or if you are buying the property for less than the lender's valuation. This can happen, for example, if you are buying your home from the council under the Right to Buy scheme at a considerable discount.

You will probably have to take out an indemnity insurance – sometimes called a mortgage guarantee policy – to cover the amount you are lent over 75 or 80 per cent. This gives the lender added security. Premiums are usually from around 3 per cent of the amount over the normal limit.

The final figure depends on the length of the mortgage and the percentage you borrow. On a 100 per cent mortgage you may pay 7 per cent or more.

If your mortgage offer is too small to buy the property you want, you may be able to raise the amount outstanding by taking out another loan from an insurance company. The interest on this top-up loan will almost certainly be higher than that on the main loan. But sometimes making up the mortgage this way can work out to be cheaper than borrowing the whole sum from one source. The reason is that some building societies and banks sometimes charge extra interest on higher percentage loans.

Once you have lived in a mortgaged property for some time and have paid back a reasonable proportion of the loan, you will have accumulated an amount of equity in the property – that is, surplus value over and above what you currently owe to the mortgage company. Better, the property may well have increased in value. For example, suppose you bought a house for £25,000, on a mortgage of £20,000. You have paid off £5,000 of the capital sum of the mortgage and the value of the house has increased by £5,000. This means you now owe £15,000 on a £30,000 house, so you have £15,000-worth of equity. Theoretically, you can take this equity in cash, if you sell up and move to another home, but most lenders, particularly building societies, will not let you do so.

If you return to your original lender simply to realise the equity by taking an extra loan, it is called a further advance. If you go to another lender, it is called a second mortgage. And if you replace the existing mortgage with a new, larger mortgage – and take the equity that way – it is called a re-mortgage. Many lenders will only offer further money this way if you are going to spend it on the house, increasing its value even further.

HOW DO I GET A MORTGAGE?

Once you have decided what type of mortgage suits your particular needs, it is time to investigate the market. If you are a first-time buyer it is also time – more than time – to start saving.

Find out which lenders favour the type of property you hope to buy – a flat or a house, old or new – and look at their terms and conditions. But keep your options open. Changes occur quickly in the mortgage market and by the time you are ready to buy, better terms may be on offer.

SAVING

You should save regularly with one or two building societies – if they are the lenders you favour. Keep your bank account in good order as well because, even if you don't take out your mortgage with the bank, the building society will probably want a reference from your bank manager. Remember too, that to buy your own home, you are going to need cash even if you obtain a 100 per cent mortgage. There are plenty of additional costs to cope with before you can move in.

It is worthwhile approaching a potential lender before you start the search for a house or flat. You may discover they can arrange a larger mortgage than you anticipated. During this visit you can also discuss the whole purchase procedure. Bank or building society staff can give you:

● information about the types of mortgages available;
● details of the tax situation relating to first time buyers;
● an estimate of the costs you will incur for solicitor's and surveyor's fees;
● the rates of stamp duty;
● details of the insurance you will need for the property;
● information on mortgage indemnity premiums.

Ask about the government's Home Loan scheme for first-time buyers. If you save with a bank or building society in the scheme for two years you could qualify for a cash bonus of £110 and an interest-free loan of £600. You need to have a minimum of £300 in your account for a year before you apply for a mortgage, and the price of your first home must not exceed a limit set by the government. This limit varies from region to region.

Next you have to go out and look for your new home. Once you have found a suitable property, make an offer subject to contract and put down a small deposit. When this has been accepted, check the building societies, banks, and insurance companies for the best offer, or, alternatively talk to a reputable mortgage broker who has access to these sources of money.

GETTING THE MORTGAGE

When you return to the mortgage lender or broker to arrange the mortgage you will need to take your cheque book (for the survey fee), your passport or birth certificate, your marriage certificate (if you are buying a property jointly with your spouse), the name and address of your current lender and the roll number of your mortgage if you already have one, or your landlord's name and address if you do not.

You will also have to provide proof of your income. This can be a letter from your employer, recent pay slips, or your Form P60. If you are self-employed the mortgage company may require a letter from your accountant, or they may want to see your books for the last three years.

You will probably need a solicitor to do the conveyancing, though it is possible to do it yourself. If you do not have a solicitor the mortgage lender may suggest one. Your solicitor can also act for them without conflict of interest.

SURVEYS

The lender will then want to value the property. You will have
to pay for this survey, and you may be advised to have one of
your own. This duplication may be annoying, especially as the
mortgage company often will not let you see the results of
their survey, even though you paid for it. If there is a major
problem they will bring it to your attention, but their survey
is intended simply for valuation. Your own survey will be
more thorough and will help you to decide whether the
house is sound and what repairs are likely to be necessary.
Your solicitor should be able to recommend a surveyor.

A full structural survey costs about £300 for a property of
about £40,000. A homebuyer's report, which is not so
comprehensive but may be adequate, costs about £150. The
mortgage company's valuation survey costs about £65 on the
same property, but costs are calculated on a scale linked to
property values.

THE OFFER

Once your status has been approved by the lender and the
property passed as satisfactory, you will receive your formal
mortgage offer. This will set out the monthly repayments and
the current interest rate. If it is not sufficient you may want to
go elsewhere, but you will have to pay for another lender's
survey. And it all takes time. You may be competing against
other buyers. But with luck – and good planning – you will
get the offer you require and the purchase can go ahead.

Nowadays it is possible to arrange a mortgage and
receive a Certificate of Mortgage Offer, usually valid for three
months but renewable, on the basis of your income; before
you find a property. This can be very useful.

CONVEYANCING

Conveyancing is the legal process of transferring the
ownership of property from one person to another. It is

possible to do the conveyancing yourself, but the great majority of home buyers hire a solicitor. The charge is normally ·75 to 1 per cent of the purchase price, but you should get quotes from several solicitors.

There are other conveyancing costs which you will also have to pay. Searches have to be made to make sure that the property does belong to the person who is selling it, that there are no special constraints on the deeds, and that the house is not about to be torn down to make way for a motorway! These searches usually cost about £15, though charges can vary.

Land registry fees and stamp duty must be paid too. Your purchase has to be registered so that you are the registered owner next time a search is made. The charge for registering a £40,000 property is about £70. Stamp duty (a government tax) is 1 per cent of the purchase price if the property costs over £25,000.

Solicitors may incur other incidental costs, but they should not amount to more than £25 or so.

CONTRACTS

When the draft contract is agreed by the solicitors representing you and the vendor – the person selling the house – you will be asked to sign it and put down a deposit, usually 10 per cent of the purchase price. If you are taking a 100 per cent mortgage the lender may help here or the solicitors may come to some helpful agreement.

The vendor also signs a copy of the contract and the two are exchanged. At this point, though not before, you are legally bound to proceed with the purchase. (In Scotland, once your 'bid' has been accepted by a vendor, you are both legally bound in a contract.) It also becomes your responsibility to insure the property. Henceforth, you are accountable for any damage. This process is normally completed four weeks after you exchange contracts.

Between the exchange of contracts and the completion date – the date the property is actually handed over – your solicitor will finalise the legal details. He or she arranges the time for handing over the keys and money – your part and the mortgage company's – to the vendor.

Then you can move in. Soon you will receive a statement from the lender giving you details of the repayments and the date of the first mortgage payment.

HOW INTEREST IS CALCULATED

On endowment or pension-linked mortgages – and all mortgages in which only the interest is paid to the lender – this is a simple matter. The lender will send you a statement of their well-publicised interest rates, which more or less follow the banks' minimum lending rates.

But with building societies' repayment mortgages, like hire-purchase loans, the interest paid varies slightly from the quoted rate. This occurs because you are paying off some of the capital month by month along with the interest. The amount owed, which you are paying interest on, is going down all the time. Unless the lender calculates interest on a daily basis, there is bound to be a discrepancy between the rate you think you are paying and what you are actually paying. But the building society is not cheating you. It is obliged to reveal exactly what the APR (*Annual Percentage Rate*) on its loan is.

INTEREST ON WHAT?

With repayment mortgages, building societies mostly charge interest on the basis of the balance owing at the end of each year. This means that if you owe £12,000 on 31 December 1988, your twelve monthly payments during 1989 will be calculated on the basis of that balance outstanding throughout the year. So, if the interest rate is 10 per cent, you will pay £100 a month in interest alone.

Banks, on the other hand, charge interest on the daily balance. They are used to doing this with overdrafts. Each monthly payment is deducted from the outstanding balance and every three months they calculate the interest owing for that period and add it to the rest. Neither system is perfect in every respect, but the banks' stated mortgage rate is closer to the true APR than a building society's.

INTEREST RATES CALCULATOR

Interest only payment per month, excluding tax relief.

	£2,500	£5,000	£10,000	£30,000
8%	16.66	33.33	66.67	200.00
9%	18.75	37.50	75.00	225.00
10%	20.83	41.67	83.33	250.00
11%	22.95	45.83	91.67	275.00
12%	25.00	50.00	100.00	300.00
13%	27.08	54.17	108.33	325.00

FIXING THE RATE

When you take out a traditional home loan, the lender reserves the right to charge you whatever interest they consider necessary. In other words you make an open-ended commitment to pay whatever interest rate the lender demands! In reality, the situation is not so unfavourable to the borrower as that suggests.

As the mortgage market is highly competitive, the lending institutions must keep their rates as low as possible. If they pushed their rates up, they would not attract new borrowers, who could get cheaper money elsewhere, and existing borrowers would start remortgaging their properties at the lower rates available from other lenders.

Until a few years ago the building societies used to fix a common interest rate by mutual agreement, but that came to be considered restrictive practice. Today, in any case, with so many new lenders in the market, it is no longer practical for a cartel to fix a rate.

In practice, lenders' mortgage rates roughly follow the rates of the money market. Many lenders get the money for mortgages by trading on the money markets, and the money market rates are fixed by international supply and demand. These days the margin between money market rates and mortgages has been reduced to about 1 per cent.

It is not practical to change the mortgage rate with every fluctuation of the money markets, and lenders only change rate when a major shift occurs. To recalculate every borrower's repayments and then notify them of the new rate is an expensive procedure.

FIXED RATES

It is possible to get a fixed rate mortgage at a rate lower than the current floating mortgage rate. Again, the rate is fixed by the lender – but for a period of, say, five years, rather than for the life of the mortgage. The lender obtains the money from the money markets, but long term money is cheaper to buy – i.e. the interest rate charged on it is lower – because the lender is guaranteed a fixed return for a longer period. In other words, there is less risk.

The mortgage lender passes this fixed rate on to the borrower at a mark-up of about 1 per cent.

LIBOR

The money market rate is called LIBOR – the *London Interbank Offered Rate*. It represents the underlying interest rates which determine the cost of borrowing money. It is often referred to as the wholesale price and is the type of funding that most lending institutions adopt. Although the interest rate that is applied to traditional home-loan mortgages is not linked to a particular standard, lending institutions generally lend at 1 per cent over the LIBOR rate for money lent for a period of three months.

But most lenders take a longer view of interest rates when gauging normal home loans, and this is not always in line with their wholesale funding. Often the borrower has to wait months for the interest rate applied to his mortgage to be changed. This is particularly disturbing if interest rates generally are moving downwards.

But you can ensure that your mortgage is directly in touch with the money markets by taking out a LIBOR-linked mortgage. Your mortgage rate would then be adjusted every three months. The margin fixed over funding varies between institutions, but 1 per cent or slightly less is normal. Obviously, the disadvantage of this arrangement is that if interest rates rise you will be paying the extra more quickly than you would with other types of mortgage.

HOW YOU PAY INTEREST

Americans often wonder why the British are prepared to take on a mortgage at an interest rate that can change at the discretion of the lender. To them this 'unfair' system appears to involve an open-ended commitment by the borrower. But things are better than they may seem.

The long tradition of building societies in the UK means that the market is not dominated by purely financial considerations. Building societies are non-profit-making organisations whose primary aim is to help people buy their own homes – though, of course, they must look after the interests of all their members, investors as well as borrowers. Nevertheless, fixed-loan mortgages are today on the increase in the UK market.

HOME LOAN RATE

This is the traditional arrangement whereby a mortgage is charged at a variable interest rate. The rate is determined by how competitive the lender wishes to be and is not linked to any particular standard; but the currently competitive market makes it unlikely that a lender will step dramatically out of line.

However, the lender's competitiveness should be assessed thoroughly. As in all cases, attention should be paid to application fees, administration costs, solicitor's charges and of course the way in which interest is calculated, all of which will have a direct bearing on the total cost of borrowing.

FIXED-RATE MORTGAGES

Lloyds Bank offered the first fixed-rate mortgage in 1986. The rate was fixed at 9.9 per cent, but was accompanied by fairly stringent conditions. Then the American giant Citibank (part of Citicorps) brought its fixed-interest experience to bear.

Its Executive Selection range of mortgages included a fixed-rate mortgage, usually guaranteeing the rate for the first five years rather than the shorter terms previously offered by other lenders; a new fixed rate can be negotiated at the end of the fixed term.

The advantages of this type of mortgage are the peace of mind of knowing exactly what the monthly payment will be and maybe a more competitive rate over the term. But there are penalties if you want to pay off your mortgage early and also, as a rule, if you convert back to a variable rate.

Some lenders, however, will offer a switch to the normal, variable, home-loan rate without penalty. This mortgage is particularly advantageous in the case of larger loans, when an unfavourable change in interest rates has a particularly severe effect on outgoings.

DROP LOCK

In addition to the fixed-rate facility some lenders also offer what is known as the drop lock. This enables the borrower to take a variable rate at first and at a later stage drop into a fixed rate. There is no penalty in this case.

INDEX-LINKED MORTGAGES

Index-linked mortgages set the mortgage rate you pay at a differential – say 6 per cent – over inflation. So when inflation is 4 per cent you pay 10 per cent. If the inflation rate falls you have a very cheap mortgage, but if it rises the mortgage becomes expensive.

Remember that the term of a mortgage is usually 20 or 25 years, and no one can see that far into the future. However, if you are confident that the rate of inflation will come down over the next five or ten years, and if, like most people, you move house during the term of the mortgage and take out a new one, then an index-linked mortgage is an option worth considering.

DEFERRED-INTEREST AND LOW-START SCHEMES

These schemes allow you to reduce your monthly repayment by deferring part of the interest repayment, through either a low-start scheme or a flexible-payment scheme allowing monthly payments to be reduced when required. The deferred interest is added to the mortgage account and on a low-start scheme additional monthly payments will be required later to reduce the outstanding debt to the original figure. There are facilities that allow for a high degree of flexibility in the increase paid to the lender, and this may be adjusted with as little as one month's notice.

The minimum low-start payment is significantly lower than the normal payment. This means that you can take out a larger loan at a lower initial payment than a conventional mortgage, provided you are confident that your income is going to rise. This is a reasonable assumption if, for instance, you are a student with firm employment prospects or a low-paid trainee in a lucrative trade.

Many people prefer to make lower-than-normal monthly payments in the early years of their mortgage, knowing that these payments will have to increase later to compensate, but calculating that by that time their income will have risen sufficiently to cope. A steadily increasing payment schedule is more logical than the traditional mortgage which, due to the effects of inflation, imposes the biggest burden at the beginning of the term, when the borrower's resources are usually smaller.

The low-start payment option is designed to start payments off about 25 per cent below normal interest payments. A proportion of the unpaid interest is deferred until later in the term of the mortgage. Payments will obviously have to increase later on to compensate for the earlier shortfall, but they are calculated to rise by only 5 per cent each year for the first 20 years of the mortgage, though you can make alternative arrangements. A 5 per cent increase every 12 months should be tolerable for most people. Average increase in earnings is more than that, and the inflation rate is not likely to be much less, so in real terms the cost of the mortgage payments does not rise.

FLEXIBLE-PAYMENT MORTGAGES

The idea of a flexible-payment mortgage is that you pay what you like – subject, of course, to a minimum set by the lender – and you can change the amount you pay as often as you like. Some joint borrowers – especially husbands and wives – want to pay more at the beginning, when they are both earning. With a flexible-payment plan, they can drop back to the minimum payment when they start a family. You can change your rate of repayment at any time – even pay the whole debt off at once if you inherit a fortune – without incurring any penalty.

LIBOR-LINKED MORTGAGES

LIBOR, the *London Interbank Offered Rate*, provides an alternative variable base for interest rates charged to borrowers by mortgage lenders. The standard rate can fluctuate quite rapidly with changes in the economy. With LIBOR-linked mortgages some of these fluctuations are ironed out.

On the last working day of each quarter, the mortgage company sets its rate at a slight premium – usually about 1 per cent – above the LIBOR rate. This rate remains fixed for the whole of the following quarter. The standard mortgage rate may go up or down, but the LIBOR-linked rate does not.

The apparent advantage of this system lies in the fact that the LIBOR rate has tended to remain slightly below the standard mortgage rate for most of the time since it was introduced. Also, fixed quarterly rates make budgeting easier.

Some lenders who offer both standard mortgages and LIBOR-linked mortgages will allow borrowers to switch between the two rates, provided 28 days notice is given before the end of the quarter. The borrower can only switch at the end of the quarter, and only one switch is allowed in each calendar year. There is usually a charge of £100 for each switch.

STABILISED PLANS

Interest rates have been known to fluctuate dramatically during the life of a mortgage. In order to overcome the inconvenience of adjusting monthly repayments, the stabilised plan has emerged as a popular mortgage facility.

The lender makes a projection of interest rates over a period of normally three years and fixes a rate at the estimated likely average over that period. This determines the borrower's repayments. However, the mortgage account is charged in accordance with an interest rate linked to the lending institution's normal home loan rate. At the end of the three-year period the mortgage account is adjusted in accordance with the rate changes, the resulting mortgage debt reflecting these changes.

CAPS AND COLLARS

At any time during the term of a mortgage it is possible to take out an insurance policy that caps the mortgage repayments. In other words, while the mortgage rate can go down, it cannot go up above a predetermined rate. For a one-off payment you buy the peace of mind of a capped interest rate.

Historically, interest rates have been known to jump very suddenly and this can have a serious effect on budgeting. When interest rates are low it may be advisable to take advantage of this capping facility. However, the cost of the cap is determined by market forces, and when interest rates are low it tends to be expensive.

A cheaper way of capping your mortgage is by buying a cap and collar. Citibank was the first to import this idea from the United States. For a payment equal to one month's interest, the borrower can cap the loan at the initial rate of interest for the first five years. If interest rates rise above that level, his payments are unaffected. However, the rate may fall, along with interest rates, down to the so-called collar rate – if they fall further the lender is the gainer.

Under this scheme, the mortgage rate can fluctuate only within a narrow band and the borrower has the security of knowing that his rate will never climb above a certain level. The disadvantage is that he does not benefit from a fall in the interest rate below the lower level.

The duration of the cap and collar is agreed at the outset. Normally it runs for up to five years, the facility being renegotiated at the end of that period.

HOW TAX RELIEF WORKS

When you buy your own home, the government offers some assistance. It allows tax relief on the interest you pay on a mortgage, and if you have a pension-linked mortgage you can claim tax relief on your pension contributions too.

HOW MUCH?

Under current arrangements, you are entitled to tax relief on the interest you pay on a mortgage loan of up to £30,000. Larger loans receive tax relief on the interest on the first £30,000 only. The money does not have to be used exclusively for purchase; tax relief is also allowed on the interest on loans taken out to make home improvements.

Married couples only qualify for the single £30,000 tax relief limit. But for an unmarried couple, each paying half the interest, the limit is twice that, and this applies even if one partner pays no tax at all.

Tax relief only applies to the principal residence. If you are buying a holiday home or a cottage for weekends in the country you will not be eligible.

MIRAS

Normally, home loans of less than £30,000 from building societies and banks qualify for the MIRAS (*Mortgage Interest Relief at Source*) scheme. This means that the building society, bank or other lender calculates the tax relief and deducts it from your payments.

If you are borrowing less than £30,000, your repayments are made after tax relief at the basic rate has been deducted, but if you pay a higher rate of income tax and you are accordingly entitled to a higher rate of tax relief, you must claim the extra from the Inland Revenue. They will adjust your tax code accordingly.

If you have borrowed more than £30,000, the interest on the first £30,000 also qualifies under MIRAS on new loans. On loans issued before 5 April 1987, some lenders decline to operate the MIRAS scheme on loans over £30,000. In that case, the homeowner has to find the full amount of the mortgage repayment and claim the tax relief back from the Inland Revenue.

MIRAS has obvious advantages for the borrower. It is straightforward, because the lender handles the details, and the tax relief is immediate. Because it does not discriminate between taxpayers and non-taxpayers, you continue to receive tax relief if you are unemployed or ill. This is a particular advantage to the self-employed, who would otherwise face delay in receiving the tax relief and might not get the full amount if their tax liability were less than the amount they would receive.

PENSION-LINKED MORTGAGES

Capital repayments on repayment mortgages are not subject to tax relief. Until 1984, it was possible to get tax relief on payments made on endowment policies and linked to endowment mortgages. Homeowners who took out endowment mortgages before then still receive tax relief on their payments made into the endowment policy. But there is no tax relief on new endowment policies.

However, payments into individual pension plans still attract tax relief. Therefore, if you take out a pension-linked mortgage, you receive tax relief on the interest you pay on the sum borrowed, and on the payments you make into the pension plan which pays back the loan at the end of the term.

WILL TAX RELIEF LAST?

Tax relief on mortgage interest payments underpins the economics of buying a home in the UK. For most people

MIRAS effectively turns an 11 per cent mortgage interest rate into one of about 8 per cent.

This important concession is often said to distort the housing market. House owners are subsidised on their mortgage payments but tenants get no tax relief on their rent. It is also said to cause house price inflation: home-buyers can afford to borrow – and thus to pay – proportionately more.

MIRAS not only makes it easier to buy a house or to afford a bigger mortgage, it also helps to increase the individual homeowner's real wealth. Tax relief means that people make a large – and tax free – real gain, as opposed to a nominal gain, on their houses.

The real capital gain is the amount you sell your house for after deducting what it has cost you over the years to buy it. The nominal capital gain is simply the difference between its sale price and what you originally paid for it. Many people think only in terms of the nominal capital gain. They argue that everybody needs somewhere to live and what they have paid in interest they would have spent on rent.

Tax relief has attracted fierce criticism from many quarters, not least the Treasury, which reckons that it now costs the government nearly £5 billion a year. Other people, especially housing groups, point out that it is an indiscriminate form of housing subsidy – not only because it is available only to those who buy rather than rent, but also because it helps the richest proportionately more than others since the tax relief is given against the borrower's top rate of income tax. Even Conservative politicians criticise it because it makes investment in housing more attractive – especially for the rich – than more economically useful investments such as industry.

Major reform of the system is nevertheless widely acknowledged to be politically problematic for the party that adopts it. Even the Labour Party, though obviously unhappy with the system, rebuts the suggestion that it has any plans to scrap mortgage interest tax relief.

Within the Conservative Party there are also many who are unhappy with the way mortgage interest tax relief works, but even its sternest critics stop short of advocating its abolition, proposing either a very gradual phasing-out of relief over 10 or 15 years or restrictions on the extent of the relief that can be claimed by new rather than existing borrowers. But Prime Minister Margaret Thatcher appears to be personally in favour, not of restricting tax relief, but of extending it.

The most likely outcome is that mortgage interest tax relief will be allowed to wither away. The limit will remain at £30,000 although that is already a relatively low level for those buying houses in London and the south east of England, where mortgages of £80,000-plus are not unusual.

There is a possibility that a government may restrict tax relief to the basic rate of tax, reducing the bias in favour of the rich. And the Inland Revenue is taking firmer action against people who increase their mortgages for alleged home improvements but spend the money on other things.

HOME IMPROVEMENTS

As explained above, tax relief on mortgage interest is only available in certain circumstances – for purchase or improvement of the home, etc. There are certain exceptions to the rules. For instance, an elderly person can claim tax relief on a home-income plan if he or she is aged 65 or more, and at least 90 per cent of the loan raised is used to buy an annuity to provide an income.

Home improvement loans can cause the biggest headache. Eligible improvements are defined as permanent alterations to the property which add to the existing accommodation or amenities. They do not include repairs, routine maintenance or decoration, unless the property was bought in a dilapidated condition and the money was used to restore it. Examples of qualifying improvements include home extensions, loft conversions, central heating, double-glazing, insulation of the roof or walls, new bathrooms, permanently fitted kitchen and bedroom units, garages, greenhouses and swimming pools.

USING MIRAS TO BUY A CAR

The Inland Revenue has recently become increasingly worried about the number of people claiming relief on false premises. To clamp down on this abuse, it has clarified the wording in MIRAS 70, the form which you must sign declaring the use to which you intend to put the loan before you can get relief, and it is conducting the occasional prosecution of tax-relief cheats. However, even the Inland Revenue admits that many people claim relief in the sincere belief that they are entitled to it when they are not.

The same rules apply whether you are seeking a further advance, a remortgage or a top-up loan – tax relief is only available on a loan, or part of a loan which is actually used for one of the specified purposes. Rather illogically, though, the Inland Revenue has no interest in capital released when you sell your house. That means that if you had a £20,000 mortgage and wanted to buy a car for £10,000 and tried to raise that amount of money by taking out a top-up loan or remortgaging, you would not get tax relief on any more than the original £20,000 figure. But you could move next door to an identically priced house and use the capital tied up in your house to buy the car – in that case, the whole £30,000 amount of the new mortgage would qualify for tax relief!

ASSESSING INTEREST RATES

Although the building societies and banks fix the interest rate paid on a mortgage, they cannot fix it at any level they choose. If they set it too high, customers will go elsewhere. Besides, the building societies are non-profit-making organisations duty-bound to help people own their homes. If they set their rate too high they would discourage people from doing that. Even commercial lenders would suffer in this event. There is a lot of money to be made on the mortgage market, but only while so many people are seeking to become home owners. No one would profit if they decide to rent instead. In any case mortgages are like any other form of investment. They depend on interest rates set by factors in the economy at large.

PUBLIC SECTOR BORROWING
The amount which the government and local authorities need to borrow on the money markets – the PSBR or *Public Sector Borrowing Requirement* – is one of the prime factors. If they want to borrow too much, they reduce the quantity of free money on the market. And if lenders lend to the Government – a borrower who is hardly likely to default on the loan – they have less money to lend to mortgage seekers.

BALANCE OF PAYMENTS
The prosperity of the country as a whole is also important. If the national economy is buoyant and the outlook promising, lenders do not mind making loans at fairly low rates – they are confident of getting their money back. However, in such a situation not everything works to the advantage of the individual borrower. If the manufacturing sector of the economy is prosperous and looking for investment, industry will be competing for the available investment funds.

THE EXCHANGE RATE

The government tries to keep the exchange rate steady, so that exporters know approximately the prices they will receive for their products. It also tries to keep it low enough to make British exports relatively cheap in foreign markets and to prevent foreign imports flooding the UK market. At the same time, the rate must be high enough to prevent the cost of the raw materials that Britain has to buy from abroad becoming prohibitively expensive. British people going abroad, who benefit from a high exchange rate, must also be kept in mind.

One way of controlling the exchange rate is by adjusting the interest rate. If British institutions offer a high interest rate, foreign investors move their money into Britain, increasing the demand for British currency and pushing its value up. If interest rates fall, the money flows out of the country again, forcing the exchange rate down.

THE MONEY SUPPLY

The amount of money you can borrow depends on how much money there is in the economy as a whole. However, no one is really sure how much that is! That perhaps explains why there are various ways of calculating it. For example, the government prints money at the Royal Mint. If it needs an extra million pounds, it can simply print it. However, this would affect the exchange rate.

That is not the only money available in the economy. Most of the money people spend is not in the form of cash but is represented by cheques, standing orders, credit cards etc. But in fact, what is borrowed through credit cards, on an overdraft, or through a department store account is a form of cash. So, to control the money supply, it is necessary to control interest rates. If the money supply seems to be dangerously large and inflationary, the government acts to raise interest rates.

INFLATION

The rate of inflation – and the inflation outlook – is a vitally important consideration to lenders. The inflation rate measures how much their money loses in value year-on-year: if, for example the interest rate is 10 per cent and the inflation rate 5 per cent, the lender is only making 5 per cent in real terms. At one point during the height of inflation in the 1970s, the inflation rate climbed above interest rates, so that lenders were in fact *losing* money by lending it. That is unlikely to happen again: when inflation climbs, so do interest rates.

PROPERTY PRICES

Your mortgage is not just an investment for the mortgage company. Because you spend it on buying property, it is an investment for you too. If property prices increase faster than interest rates, you will make a profit.

If the property you have bought increases in value by 20 per cent a year and you are paying 10 per cent interest, you are making 10 per cent a year on what you have borrowed. But a mortgage is more complicated than that. Suppose you have a with-profit endowment policy: you are also making money on that policy as you pay into it because the money is being invested on your behalf by the insurance company. Your total profit is therefore well over 10 per cent.

PERSONAL INCOME

Another factor working to the adantage of the homeowner is rising income. Many homeowners did very well during the high inflation of the 1970s. Their incomes rocketed and so did the value of their property, while the amount they owed stayed the same, or declined, during the term of the mortgage. Even in times of low inflation, people who take on what they think is a worryingly large mortgage to start with often find that, after a few years, the repayments have become relatively trivial compared with their advancing salary.

FUTURE TRENDS

Forecasting the future for the world economy is a notoriously hazardous occupation. Things can change so quickly. But there is no sign that the high inflation of the last decade is likely to return. There are Third World countries who cannot re-pay their debts, but banks have found ways to reschedule and write off debts without seriously disrupting the international money markets – or interest rates.

Interest rates seem likely to remain stable, or to decline slightly, in the foreseeable future. But political factors, wars, nuclear accidents and acts of God may disrupt all forecasts.

CASHING IN

Your home is probably your biggest single asset. That's why house prices are such a constant topic of conversation. Everybody wants to know how much more their house is worth today than yesterday, and how much more it is going to be worth tomorrow.

Every month a plethora of statistics on house prices is published. But for some time now the message has been the same. House prices nearly everywhere are rising comfortably above the rate of inflation, currently about 15 per cent a year, and there is no end in sight.

CAN IT LAST?

No one is keen to predict how long this rate of increase will continue. Even the most pessimistic see only a slowdown rather than a sharp reversal.

Despite unemployment, the incomes of those in work are still rising ahead of inflation. Traditionally, there is a close link between incomes and house prices: when people earn more, they naturally have more to spend on houses. High incomes fuel the rise in house prices.

In each of the past 32 years average house prices have invariably risen. In only nine years have they risen by less than inflation. Indeed in real terms – that is, after taking account of inflation – they have increased in value more than eightfold since 1955.

Some people still mutter darkly about a crash. It can't go on, they say, and they make vague references to the 'property crash' of the mid-1970s. However, only commercial property fell seriously in value at that time. House prices held steady against inflation.

House prices peaked in 1973, when they rose by 42.4 per cent. Inflation at that time was 7.7 per cent. The next year they

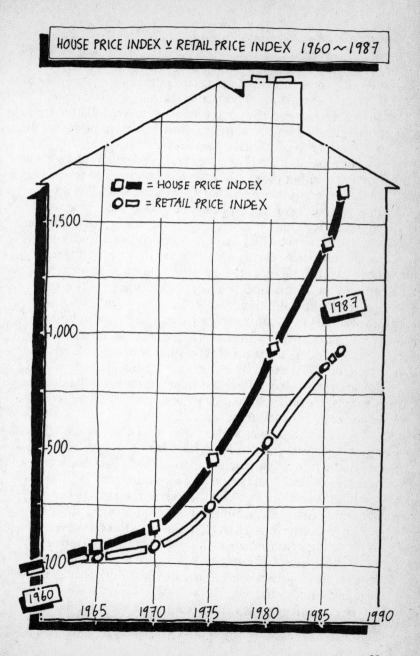

HOUSE PRICE INDEX v RETAIL PRICE INDEX 1960~1987

☐ ■ = HOUSE PRICE INDEX
○ ▭ = RETAIL PRICE INDEX

1,500

1,000

1987

500

100

1960

1965   1970   1975   1980   1985   1990

63

still outstripped inflation, rising 15.4 per cent compared with 10.3 per cent inflation. Then came the slump, and in the following four years the position was reversed: inflation rose more quickly than house prices. Even so, it was not enough to wipe out the gains of the two previous years.

Underpinning the continuing rise in property values is the growing number of people who want a house. This number is likely to continue to rise for a few more years. Yet the supply of new housing, especially in areas of highest demand, will be increasingly restricted by the scarcity of land. That is one of the factors which has given rise to the notorious north-south price divide. Not only are people in the south more likely to be in work and earning money, there are also more of them chasing a roughly static number of houses.

The Halifax Building Society figures provide yet more proof of this now familiar pattern. House prices in July 1987 rose rapidly in the south-east of England, where they went up by 22.9 per cent a year, and slowly in the north of England, where they increased by 7.9 per cent. The only place where house prices increased by less than the rate of inflation was Northern Ireland, where they were falling by 2.8 per cent a year, a very unusual situation.

Some estate agents and economists have assumed that this means prices in the south have become 'overheated', and that, while house prices nationally will not collapse, they may do so locally in London and the south east.

It has been pointed out that while the price gap between north and south has been widening since the beginning of 1982, back in 1971, the position was reversed. In those days house prices in London and the south-east were increasing by only 1 or 2 per cent a year, and the fastest rate of growth was in the north, where prices were rising at 4 per cent a year.

House prices were sluggish at the time, and so it has been argued that although prices in London and the south-east may grow faster than in other areas in good times, the position is reversed in slack years, when the rest of the country catches up. All in good time, they say, the tide will turn.

However, the Nationwide Building Society recently produced some calculations, showing that the catching-up process falls short. Overall, the south-east creeps ahead. Over the past twelve years prices in London and the south-east have increased more than fivefold, while in the north and the West Midlands they have merely tripled.

There are some regional economic bright spots like Chester which have been successful in attracting new industry and where house prices have risen accordingly. And in time, perhaps, the economic boom in the south may gradually extend to the Midlands and the north. But most economists now agree that the trend is probably irreversible. The economic axis of the country has shifted permanently towards the south-east, with its proximity to Europe. What may happen is that a few very high-priced areas within central London will suffer over the next year or so; or more likely, a few people who have bought properties in new luxury developments at inflated prices will find it difficult to sell at a profit.

A much more likely development is that London prices will spread out from the centre, with house prices in areas around London rising fastest. A recent Halifax survey provides strong evidence that this ripple effect is already happening. For the first time during the current price boom, London house prices were actually outstripped by an adjacent region – East Anglia.

It is, of course, first-time buyers who underpin the market. If they can't afford to buy their first house, others cannot move up the chain. Until recently it was thought that house prices in London were reaching a level that first-time buyers could not afford and that this would act as a brake on the market. This did not happen and the Halifax concluded on the basis of their research that first-timers were finding a variety of ways around the problem. In particular, they were clubbing together to buy flats: more than 70 per cent of buyers had more than one income to support their mortgage.

This double-income phenomenon has been one of the most important factors keeping the market buoyant – after all, two people can live in virtually the same space as one, but can afford to pay twice the price for it.

Another factor has been a London version of the ripple effect. A survey by the London Research Centre showed that buyers at the bottom end of the market were buying predominately in the cheapest areas, such as Newham, Croydon, Waltham Forest, Barking and Wandsworth.

All this suggests that house prices will continue to rise faster than inflation for a short period but that, particularly in central London, the rate at which prices are rising will stabilise. Meanwhile the gap between London and surrounding areas such as those around Reading, Swindon, Cambridge and Norwich will narrow, as will the gap between highly priced London boroughs and cheaper ones. But the fundamental gap between the south and the north will continue to widen, with the possible exception of a few cities such as Chester and Manchester.

REALISING THE EQUITY

Bearing these facts in mind, it is clear that many people, especially those living in the south, are in possession of a small fortune in the shape of their family house. However, it will probably have to remain a fortune on paper only. We cannot simply sell up and enjoy the money. We all have to live somewhere, and most of us become fond of our accustomed life-style and environment. Also, if we do sell, and thus jump off the house-price ladder, we may never be able to climb back on it, as we no longer have a valuable property to trade.

Yet selling up and moving is by far the best way to get at the paper wealth. Any other mechanism for raising cash against the value of a property is going to cost money. The sad truth is that all those in the business of lending money want to make money themselves – and they can only do that by charging the borrowers one way or another.

If you do want to release some of the capital tied up in your house, you should first at least consider 'trading down' i.e. buying a cheaper property – a smaller house in the same area or an equivalent house in a cheaper area.

Most people move house within a 10-mile radius. That can mean missed opportunities to make money by buying a cheaper home in an area slightly further away but likely to appreciate faster than other areas. It is worth being a little more adventurous. Watch for signs of the 'gentrification' of run-down areas, which may also offer a chance of buying and renovating a period property which would normally be outside your reach. Signs to look for are a great deal of building activity, lots of skips in the roads, improved communications – perhaps a new road which will make the area more accessible.

Alternatively, consider moving to a smaller property. That might not sound appealing, but when you investigate the market you may be surprised at what is available.

If you are lucky enough to live in one of the regions where house prices are high, you should consider moving into an area where prices are low. There are two possible snags here. You have to be sure of finding work and you must also ensure that you can move back to a higher-priced area if you should need to in the future. These are not necessarily insoluble problems.

For some people there is a possibility of buying a job with the home. Over 80 per cent of the purchase price of a pub, newsagent or sub-post office is made up of the value of the property. Moreover, the value of such businesses has appreciated faster than average house prices over recent years.

If you do decide to move to a cheaper region, look for areas where the local economy is buoyant. The local economy of Chester, for example, is booming and house prices there are climbing at well over the average rate. Cheltenham, which is an expensive area of the south, has been so successful in attracting new financial service industries that house prices there are outstripping those in neighbouring towns.

Picking the right area – one where, ideally, house prices are low, but the rate of house price inflation is disproportionately high – is vital if you want to move on again. The equity you put into a house there will appreciate faster than average, so even if you have skimmed off some of the equity in the move, you will soon be climbing up the ladder again.

Bear in mind that, since tax relief makes a house one of the best investments available, 'trading up', i.e. buying a more expensive house and not taking any of the equity out – may be sensible too. An investment in a London house appreciates faster than the *Financial Times* All-Share index even when the stock market is at its most bullish. Moreover you receive no tax relief on money borrowed to buy shares, nor does the share-buyer enjoy the homeowner's exemption from capital gains tax.

If you do not want to move house, however, there are other alternatives. You can borrow against the value of your house in one of several ways:

● you can ask your current lender to give you an additional loan on top of your existing mortgage,

● you can arrange a top-up loan with a different lender who will give you a second mortgage on the basis of the equity vested in the house,

● or you can remortgage your house with a new lender. This will give you the money to pay off the current loan and you can take the equity in cash. Or, if your house has appreciated in value, you can remortgage it for a higher amount to give you additional cash. But you may lose tax relief advantages, and a remortgage may not be prudent if you have a fixed-interest mortgage, which often imposes a penalty for early redemption.

Further advances and top-up loans may attract a higher rate of interest – as much as 2 per cent higher and, with a further advance, some lenders try to extract a higher rate of interest on the whole mortgage, not just the additional amount. Now that building societies can make unsecured loans up to £5,000, you may be urged to adopt this alternative. Such loans are not secured against the value of your house and the rate of interest is much higher.

FURTHER ADVANCE OR REMORTGAGE?

The answer to this question depends on how much you want to borrow and how happy you are with your existing mortgage. Since building societies have now lost their exemption from the Consumer Credit Act, many have stopped giving further advances for less than £15,000 because of the costs of administration.

A mortgage loan is still one of the cheapest means of borrowing and it may be worth consolidating your debts in one new mortgage. By borrowing a larger sum you can liquidate credit-card bills and other short-term loans. Some people are reluctant to adopt this course because a mortgage loan extends for such a long period, but as people move house on average every four or five years that is also the average life of a mortgage.

A remortgage costs more to arrange than a further advance. It involves legal and possibly administrative fees as well as the cost of a new survey, and your existing lender may impose a cancellation penalty – though few now ask for more than three months' notice of your intention to repay the outstanding debt. If the additional amount you want to borrow is more than 80 per cent of the value of the house, you will probably have to pay an insurance premium also. The total cost may be more than £500, whereas a further advance should cost substantially less than £100.

However, by swapping mortgages you may be able to get a lower rate of interest. It is often possible to save 0.75 per cent or more on your mortgage interest rate by shopping around, and with a remortgage you are usually not in such a hurry as you were when you were buying the property. The reduced interest may save you enough in the first year to cover the cost of the remortgage.

If you want to borrow more than £80,000, some brokers have schemes in which all the costs of the remortgage are paid by the new lender. In that case the remortgage costs you nothing at all!

FOR THE ELDERLY

A number of ways of realising the capital tied up in their home are open to the elderly only. There are, for example, house-reversion schemes, in which the property is sold to a financial institution at a discount on its market price. The size of the discount depends on the age of the individual – the younger he or she is, the bigger the discount. In return, the vendor receives a lump sum and the right to retain possession of the property indefinitely.

Such schemes are fine in principle, but there is little choice available and the discounts involved are usually very large. For example, the maximum amount payable for the property is usually 55 per cent. For someone aged 60 it may be as little as 35 per cent.

Some points should be borne in mind when considering such schemes. Firstly, what will happen if you die early? Some schemes will return a proportion of the discount they deducted to your estate. Secondly, is it possible to move house under the same agreement? Thirdly, will the capital sum be sufficient? You can only sell once, but some schemes allow for an extra payment later under certain conditions. Finally, although you will become a tenant in your own home, you will still be responsible for maintenance and repairs. Will you be able to afford it? A useful fact sheet available from Age Concern discusses the pros and cons of these schemes.

A better scheme for the elderly is probably one of the various home-income plans offered by many building societies and other major lenders. In effect this is a form of interest-only, low-cost remortgage. Under the Abbey National's scheme, for example, provided you are over 70 (a married couple must have a combined age of more than 150), you can take out a new mortgage on your house for up to 65 per cent of it value, provided that the loan is between £15,000 and £30,000. The Abbey National pays the money to the Royal Insurance Company which provides you with a regular monthly income, or annuity. You pay the society only the interest on the loan; the capital is repaid by the annuity policy when you die or the house is sold. The interest is always, of course, much less than the annuity.

One final suggestion for the elderly: if you live in a large house and you don't want to leave, it may be worth converting part of your house into a flat. A reputable local builder or developer may be prepared to do the work in return for a share of the profit when the flat is sold.

REMORTGAGING

A remortgage is not a second mortgage, nor is it a further advance. In the mortgage business, it is called a complete refinancing package. Its advantage over other ways of exploiting the equity earned on a property – second mortgages and further advances – is that it leaves only one charge against the property.

WHERE TO OBTAIN ONE

Most lenders will consider remortgaging your property, but they may enforce the condition that the additional money borrowed must qualify for tax relief. A qualifying loan is one taken out to buy or improve your residence, or to repay an existing loan which was originally taken out for that purpose. If your first mortgage company won't give you a remortgage, there are many others in the mortgage market who offer very competitive terms.

The Mortgage Corporation, the Household Mortgage Corporation, the Bank of Scotland and most building societies all offer remortgages on fully qualifying loans. For part-qualifying loans, there is the Canadian Imperial Bank of Commerce, Chemical Bank and Bank of Ireland Mortgages. These are mainly arranged through intermediaries such as insurance companies. For a completely nonqualifying loan, these lenders will occasionally help, as will some of the smaller building societies. For the best possible deal, the ordinary individual would probably do best to consult a financial adviser familiar with the mortgage market.

HOW A REMORTGAGE WORKS

Suppose you have a mortgage of £30,000 at an interest rate of 11.25 per cent. You want to make home improvements costing about £8,000, and you have heard that one of the newer banks on the mortgage market is offering an interest rate of only 10.9 per cent. Your existing lender would charge you at least 11.25 per cent on any additional loan – especially if the loan is on non-essential improvements, such as building a swimming pool.

A remortgage is also cheaper than taking a second mortgage for the cost of the improvements only, through a second mortgage company, and it is cheaper than taking a personal loan or an overdraft through a bank.

However, there are other considerations. The monthly payments you make on a remortgage are certainly cheaper, but the initial costs are high. You must anticipate at least another £200 to register the new first charge against the property, another valuation fee, and possiby early redemption penalties when you pay off the first mortgage.

On a further advance, by comparison, you would probably have to pay a maximum of £75 in legal fees plus, possibly, a re-inspection fee of your home for about £37.50 and, of course, no early redemption charges.

A second mortgage, when your existing lender remains the same and an additional mortgage is taken from a different lender, is not a suitable alternative in the circumstances. The Consumer Credit Act imposes rules on loans of less than £15,001 and in any event, interest rates jump by about 4 per cent on smaller loans. A second mortgage should really only be considered when a fairly substantial amount is at issue and when the existing loan is charged at a particularly advantageous rate of interest.

Not all remortgages are required for home improvements. The requirement can be to raise money to purchase a car or boat, to acquire a second home, to pay school fees or to finance a new business.

Some objectives are not acceptable. Lenders will definitely not help support an ailing business or repay another lender because you have financial problems and are in arrears on your mortgage payments. However, there is a lender for most purposes.

These days most remortgage lenders offer split MIRAS – that means you pay interest net of tax relief on the first £30,000 (or £60,000 if you are an unmarried couple), as long as at least £30,000 of the money required qualifies, with the balance paid gross. The main advantages in taking a remortgage are that you can usually anticipate a 25-year term and the interest charged is usually no higher than the rate on an existing mortgage.

If you are buying a holiday home which would be let except during the annual family holiday, currently you might have to pay an interest rate of 12.75 per cent, with the holiday home as security and a term of 20 years at the very most. On a remortgage, however, the interest rate might be only about 11 per cent, a 25-year term would be probable, and the holiday home would be unencumbered by charges.

WHAT TYPE OF MORTGAGE?

When considering a remortgage, you should ask yourself whether a different type of mortgage would suit you better. Perhaps a fixed-rate mortgage might be better this time. If you need to cut current outgoings, you might be able to arrange a deferred-interest mortgage. If your first mortgage was a straight repayment mortgage, on which you repay mainly interest for the first seven years, and if you move – like the average – once every five years or so, you may end up paying off practically no capital at all.

If you do not have the time and energy to conduct your own market research, consult a broker. Otherwise, begin looking at *Blay's* monthly mortgage tables – most libraries have a copy. It lists all the lenders, their rates, terms and conditions, and the various types of mortgage available. An alternative would be to look at one of the regular monthly magazines, such as *Mortgage Magazine*.

TIMESHARES

A remortgage is an interesting proposition if you are considering purchasing an overseas property – in Spain perhaps. Taking the overseas property as security means approaching Spanish banks for the finance. They will probably propose a maximum of 50 per cent of the valuation, charge you a higher interest rate than in the UK, and limit your borrowing to ten years. So, the only disadvantage of remortgaging to acquire the cash in this situation is that you are increasing the borrowing on your principal residence, which may seem well worthwhile.

DRAW DOWN

One of the most interesting aspects of the remortgage is the delayed draw down facility which is especially useful if you are raising the money to pay school fees, or to make home improvements over an extended period of time. This means that the extra money taken in remortgage can be borrowed – or drawn-down – if and when you need it.

The mortgage facility letter is issued for the full amount, say £80,000. If £45,000 is required to repay the existing lender and £5,000 for school fees, then you have the facility to draw down a further £30,000. You then pay interest only on this first £50,000 and the interest payment does not increase until you draw down further amounts. The following year you might build a new garage, costing £4,000, and pay school fees of £6,000, so you withdraw a further £10,000 and start paying the additional interest on this. And so on.

NEW BUSINESSES

Another popular use for remortgage money is to set up a new business. For example, Mr Brown, a publisher, is earning a good income and Mrs Brown wants to resume work as a book illustrator, but with young children she cannot yet work full time out of the home. She decides to set up on her own. Mr Brown's comfortable income can support extra payments on new finance. There is adequate equity in the property, and the lender is willing to make a new loan.

The lender's attitude would obviously be different if both Mr and Mrs Brown were going into the new business, with no other source of income. The solution in that case might be a non-status loan. Here the rules are slightly different. Most lenders will only consider a maximum loan of 70 per cent – occasionally 75 per cent – of valuation and many charge a loading on the interest rate for this type of loan.

Although income does not have to be confirmed, you must be sure you will be able to afford the monthly repayments and that your future income will attain an adequate level. You must also have an impeccable reference from your existing lender and a clear credit check with no County Court or other judgements registered against you.

EARLY REDEMPTION

Remortgages can be used for a wide variety of purposes, with tax relief available on a portion of the loan. This may involve some charges, one of which may possibly be an early redemption penalty. Fortunately, most lenders now do not make a charge if you are selling your property and buying another, even if you are not taking your next mortgage from them.

On remortgages, banks are far less flexible. Many charge as much as three months' interest when you repay your loan and will not accept notice in lieu of this interest. The major building societies, by and large, make no early payment charge, although smaller societies may charge £30, plus three days' interest, for early redemption on all their mortgages.

SECURED CREDIT LINE

The secured credit line is available to those who do not require a particularly high percentage advance in relation to the value of the property which they are purchasing or remortgaging. It is designed for the more established home owner.

As the name suggests, the facility gives a credit line, which can be drawn upon at a later stage, in addition to the mortgage outstanding. For example, if the valuation of the property was £100,000 and the existing mortgage is £30,000 the borrower may draw upon a maximum of £40,000, i.e. 70 per cent of the total valuation – the normal limit for this type of facility, though some lenders will exceed it. The interest rate applied on the main mortgage would be competitive, but the rates charged on the additional borrowings would be loaded by approximately 1 per cent. The credit facility can usually be drawn on with a cheque book and a minimum amount, perhaps £1,000, could be drawn at any time.

This type of facility is particularly attractive to those who anticipate a potential borrowing requirement for such things as school fees or share purchase, but there is not normally any stipulation as to how the money is used.

TOP-UP LOANS AND ADVANCES

A top-up loan means a second mortgage, or a loan made by a third party when another lender has registered a first charge against the property. There is actually no limit to the number of mortgages you can have on a property. Each lender protects himself against default by attaching himself to the property, which each can require to be sold, if payments have not been received, in order to recover his funds.

Second mortgages have a very poor reputation, for the most part deservedly. They are associated with high rates of interest and memories of practices which fortunately have now been outlawed. Yet for someone wanting to borrow more money they can represent an easy and often a cheap form of borrowing.

The expression 'top-up' is normally used of a second mortgage granted by an insurance company. The insurance companies are major providers of second mortgage funds and they do so on terms which, superficially at any rate, look extremely attractive. Basically, they lend over the same number of years as the first mortgage underneath them – usually a building society mortgage. The interest rate is about 2 per cent more than that charged by a first lender.

Insurance companies are keen to encourage people to use either their endowment or pension contract as the method of repaying the capital of not only their loan but also the preceding loan. If that presents no problem, then you can exploit this way of obtaining relatively cheap money. But while, in the majority of cases, the endowment or pension route is the right way to proceed, it isn't always so. The effect of taking on an unwanted policy can have a huge effect on the package, suddenly making it very expensive.

Why, then, do people take out top-up mortgages? There are many reasons but probably the most common are these:

the principal lender is not prepared to lend as much money as the borrower wants, or the lender is not prepared to lend the maximum percentage of the purchase price or valuation.

In these situations the insurance company takes on the riskiest part of the loan, when the principal lender is unwilling to lend more money based on the applicant's income, or has declined to exceed a prudent percentage advance.

Within the insurance companies there is always a battle between the investment department, which dislikes the top-up concept and the risk involved, and the marketing department, which realises that this is a promising method to increase sales. As a generalisation, the better the insurance company, the less keen it is to lend money on top-ups. Normally, such companies restrict this kind of business to clients referred by a small list of professional 'introducers'.

For those who thus have access to the top insurance companies, the terms are very attractive. They obtain relatively cheap finance, and the large income-multiple formula coupled with a good policy makes it a first-class package.

The difference between one insurance company and another is immense, but this is rarely appreciated by someone outside the field. Consider for example, two 25-year endowment policies taken out in 1961. By 1986 the same investment in each would have produced £13,482 with one and £7,723 with the other. Historic examples do not guarantee future results, and the effect of terminal bonuses on recent maturities must also be considered, but these differences do make instructive reading and a company's past performance can easily be checked in most financial magazines.

BRIDGING THE GAP
When you are trying to raise the money to buy your home, the top-up route is a useful one to help bridge the gap between purchase price and what your first lender will provide.

Where, for reasons perhaps of health or age, the top-up route is inappropriate the so-called 'second mortgage market' must be considered more closely. The traditional lenders are finance companies which normally lend at higher rates, clearing banks, which normally lend over shorter periods (usually five to seven years), and one or two first class, second mortgage lenders who are prepared to lend on terms practically identical to the first mortgage, i.e. over the same number of years and at approximately the same rate. Unfortunately there are not many of these lenders, although new legislation allowing building societies to lend on second mortgages should bring about changes in this area which can only benefit the consumer.

The position for those who wish to borrow money after they have purchased a property becomes even more complicated. Rising house prices have meant that most people's loans, which were probably at a maximum at the time of purchase, are now less than the value of the property. In the early years various other forms of credit were probably fully exploited – whether to improve the property, furnish it or merely for living expenses. After some time, when the property has appreciated in value, it is possible to consolidate these payments and perhaps raise more money still.

However, if you have a policy to cover an existing loan, then a top-up involving another insurance company needs careful consideration, since it could entail taking out a new policy in place of an existing one which is rarely a good move.

MORTGAGES ON SECOND HOMES

The economic outlook suggests that the housing market will remain buoyant in the immediate future. This may be the time to buy a little place in the country. Renting it out in the summer months can make it a profitable and enjoyable investment.

TAX RELIEF

Under normal circumstances, second homes do not qualify for tax relief: the Inland Revenue is only prepared to subsidise mortgage interest on the principal residence. But tax relief can still be obtained on second homes. And, unlike that on the main residence, it is not confined to the interest on the first £30,000 of borrowed money. The full amount can be written off, either against profits, or – more importantly – against income if the property qualifies as a furnished holiday letting.

To qualify as furnished holiday accommodation the property must meet certain conditions. It must be situated in the United Kingdom and must be let on a commercial basis. It must be available for letting for at least 140 days during the tax year and must actually be let for at least 70 days. In addition, during any seven-month period the property should not normally be in the same occupation for a continuous period of more than 31 days.

If these conditions are satisfied, the tax man will write off the full cost of mortgage interest against income. Furthermore, tax relief on second homes does not affect any entitlement to relief on the main residence. But it is not covered by MIRAS and must be arranged through PAYE or Schedule D.

The tax inspector will, of course, want to know the full details of letting arrangements.

CAPITAL ALLOWANCES

Other valuable forms of tax relief are available because income from furnished holiday lettings enjoys certain benefits by virtue of being taxed as trading income.

First, you can claim capital allowances on any items of plant and machinery you buy for the house. 'Plant and machinery' is a conveniently wide term: it would normally include items such as carpets, curtains and furniture as well as fixtures and fittings.

Another attractive feature of furnished holiday accommodation is that the rental is treated as earned income. If it is held in the wife's name, her earned-income relief is available. Further, if the rent is substantial, it may be worth making an election for separate taxation, in order to make use of the wife's basic-rate tax band. This compares favourably with other rental or investment income, which is always taxed at the husband's highest marginal rate of tax, even if the income belongs to his wife.

And there are capital gains tax advantages. In particular, a capital gain arising on the disposal of a property will be eligible for what is called 'roll-over' relief, which means that any liability to tax may be deferred indefinitely. The only condition is that a replacement asset must be bought within a period beginning the year before and ending three years after the property is sold. The replacement asset must be used for the purposes of a trade carried on by the vendor but need not necessarily be a replacement holiday property. If the property is given away, capital gains hold-over relief will be available on the gift.

Perhaps the most important advantage of furnished holiday accommodation is that it qualifies as a business asset for capital gains retirement relief. Provided you are aged over 60 or are retiring on the grounds of ill health, and have owned the property for at least one year before the date of sale, some measure of retirement relief will be available.

There is little doubt that holiday accommodation is now an attractive proposition from a tax point of view, especially as second homes are generally used only for a month or two every year by their owners. But the would-be landlord should be warned of two potential snags. Firstly, the tenants may not treat the property with the care and respect which the owner desires. Secondly, there is a danger of creating a protected tenancy under the Rent Acts.

It is also possible to claim tax relief if a relative stays in the property, but they must pay a commercial rent, they won't be allowed to stay there for the whole of the qualifying period, and they must move out after 31 days.

FINANCING THE PURCHASE

Traditionally, building societies have not been eager for second home business, especially where letting is involved. The banks are usually more accommodating and, in the current climate, there should be little difficulty in finding a suitable lender to advance the necessary funds.

INSURANCE PROTECTION

Responsibility for insuring a property naturally falls on the owner. Confusion sometimes arises because building societies, banks and other lenders often arrange building insurance for you when you take out the mortgage. That is simply a matter of convenience: many lenders, even if they are not insurance companies themselves, have special arrangements with insurance companies. You don't have to insure through them but if you don't, you will have to provide them with evidence that you are insured for the full rebuilding cost and you might have to pay an administration fee.

BUILDING INSURANCE

From the lender's point of view this is the most important insurance. It protects his security – your home.

Most policies cover loss or damage caused by the standard perils of fire, theft, storm and flood. In addition most policies offer insurance against damage caused by lightning, earthquake, vandalism, riots (but maybe not if the house is left unfurnished and unguarded for a long time), subsidence, collision, oil leakage, falling trees, etc. The cost of alternative accommodation, if the house is destroyed, will be covered up to a certain limit.

To increase protection against unforeseen mishaps, accidental damage insurance provides even wider cover. As a general guide to the cost of this insurance, estimate on £1.80 per £1,000 of cover for standard building insurance and £2.10 per £1,000 of cover for standard plus accidental damage insurance.

In each case, premiums can be reduced by as much as 30p per £1,000 if you are prepared to pay an excess, i.e. the first £50 (the usual sum) of any claim. Naturally, different insurance companies word their contracts differently. Always read the policy carefully and make sure you know exactly what you are covered against.

Cover will normally include liability insurance, in case of damage or personal injury as a result of your negligence. The sum insured should be between £250,000 and £500,000.

HOW MUCH TO INSURE FOR

You must insure your house for the full cost of rebuilding, not forgetting any out-buildings. Unfortunately, the market value of the house won't necessarily be an adequate guide to the rebuilding cost. A simple way to work out this cost for yourself is to calculate the overall area of your house in square feet, then multiply this by the average cost of rebuilding. Prices vary between £32 and £60 per square foot, depending on the type of house, its age and location. Older houses are more expensive to rebuild; rebuilding is more expensive in London, and so on.

For example, an average Victorian terraced house covers about 1,350 square feet. In south-east England, rebuilding costs are about £54 a square foot, so the overall cost would be about £54,000, (including an allowance of approximately £1,850 for central heating). This may be considerably more than the house cost to buy. For an older house requiring specialised restoration a professional valuation is advisable.

Up-to-the-minute guidance on rebuilding costs can be obtained from either the Association of British Insurers or the Royal Institution of Chartered Surveyors.

MORTGAGE PROTECTION INSURANCE

If you have a repayment mortgage and die before you have repaid it, your dependants will be saddled with the debt unless you have adequate life assurance. If you have an endowment mortgage, you are of course covered because the policy includes life assurance cover.

Some lenders, especially banks, insist on a mortgage-protection policy which will automatically pay off the mortgage if one of the borrowers dies. Normally this provides cheap protection – between £2 and £15 a month for single people, £3.50 and £23 a month for couples, on a 25-year £30,000 mortgage. The price depends on your age, health and habits, such as whether you smoke. But prices can be much higher if you are a higher-than-average risk because of your job, your leisure activities or your medical history. You must give the insurer all relevant information even if not asked directly, otherwise they may not pay out.

More favourable rates may be obtainable through a trade union or similar association.

Policies also state the maximum interest rate at which cover operates. If interest rates go up, you may not be covered for the whole amount of the outstanding loan.

Some policies allow you to increase your cover at a future date without the latest information about your health. This can be useful if you take out a bigger mortgage later when your health may not be so good. However, once you have passed a certain age you may not be able to increase cover.

MORTGAGE REDUNDANCY POLICIES

If you lose your job, mortgage redundancy policies make your mortgage repayments for up to two years. Some policies also cover the repayments if you are unable to work through accident or sickness.

CONTENTS INSURANCE

The contents of your house – from the carpets and curtains to the crockery and cutlery – need to be covered in the same way as the buildings. Most policies specify the same hazards as for building insurance and again the cover can be broadened to include accidental damage and theft.

The best policies are the index-linked 'replacement as new' type in which, with certain exceptions, the insurance company makes no deductions even for wear and tear.

Normal contents values are about £11,000 for a flat or small bungalow, £13,000 for a terraced house or larger bungalow, £16,000 for a detached house or large semi-detached or town house, and £20,000 for a large detached house.

Those are only guidelines. For a more precise estimate you must go round the house room by room adding up the cost of replacing each item. The total often seems horrifyingly high. But your insurance must protect you against the worst eventuality, such as fire that destroys everything in the house. Any very valuable items – worth over £500 – should be listed separately; the insurance company may require an independent valuation.

HIGH-RISK ITEMS

There are certain articles which are known in the business as high-risk items and if you have many of them – especially if their value exceeds one-third of the total value of the contents – you may have to pay a slightly higher premium. Among high-risk items are jewellery, paintings, television sets, radios, stereo equipment, video recorders, cameras, clocks and watches, computers and fur coats. Objects often removed from the house which must be insured wherever they are (cameras, jewels, fur coats, etc.) should be covered under a separate personal property all-risks section and not included in the house-contents sum insured.

THE COSTS

Contents insurance costs vary enormously from one part of the country to another, and between city and rural areas.

In parts of London the average cost is currently about £12.50 per £1,000 of the sum assured. In the suburbs, it is about £5.00 per £1,000 and in country areas it can be as low as £3 per £1,000. You can usually reduce the cost by about 50p per £1,000 of cover if you are prepared to pay the first £50 of any claim yourself. All-risk insurance costs more, but it is probably worth covering expensive items which you intend to take out of the house.

BRIDGING LOANS AND CHAINBREAKING

More than 1 million people move house every year in England and Wales, but not all moves go smoothly. The greatest source of problems is the buying and selling chain that is set up, with every vendor dependent on his purchaser. Until you nail 'sold' on a 'for sale' sign you remain hostage to the weakest link in the chain.

These problems rarely occur in Scotland as once an offer is made and accepted the transaction is legally binding. This leaves no room for either party to back out of the deal or delay completion.

In most successful moves in England and Wales, the crucial factor is the timing of exchange of contracts and of sale and purchase. Many have experienced the nightmare of a broken chain, when the buyer of their old home backs out at the last minute and leaves them with the prospect of losing the house they were about to buy. Others have found themselves in a race to sign a contract. Some, having been successful at auction and being obliged to exchange contracts immediately, have been unable to complete their purchase because the equity was tied up in their old home.

One answer is to borrow the money required to buy your new home as a bridging loan, which is repayable on the eventual sale of the old home. Another is to make a quick sale of your old home to a chainbreaker.

Each alternative costs something. Bridging loans inevitably attract interest. Chainbreaking entails the property being sold at a sizeable discount from the price a willing buyer might pay. However, this is not to imply that either is without merit.

First, you effectively become a cash buyer. A seller normally prefers an offer which is not conditional on the sale of the buyer's old home, and as a cash buyer you are in a position to agree a deal more quickly. This may enable you to negotiate a sizeable cash discount.

You can also decide when to move. Knowing when you will be able to complete your purchase – before your sale if necessary – you can move precisely when you wish and avoid the panic of moving out of the old home and into the new one on the same day.

The flexibility this gives you also increases the chance of buying exactly what you want. You can start looking at prospective properties at any time, and need not place your old home on the market until you have found your ideal new one.

In the search for a problem-free move, chainbreaking schemes certainly have a place. However, you may have to pay a discount of between 7.5 and 12.5 per cent of the property's realistic value for a quick sale, and for this reason they should only really be considered as a last resort.

BRIDGING LOANS

A bridging loan, while it may not give the seller the same peace of mind until the property is sold, will most probably cost less than a chainbreaker. There are two types of bridging loan: closed – for those who have exchanged on both their sale and purchase but must complete the purchase first; and open – for those who have exchanged on their purchase but have yet to exchange on the sale.

The need for both types of loan arises constantly. Banks are normally willing to grant their clients closed bridging loans. They may grant open bridging loans but only in circumstances where they can be assured that the property is likely to be re-sold fairly quickly, that the client has a fairly substantial equity in the house he or she is selling, and that the borrower would be able to pay the interest on the bridging loan if the property were not to sell for a considerable time.

Interest on a bridging loan is normally charged on a quarterly basis. It is negotiable at around 3 to 3·5 per cent over the bank's base rate. Bank base rates are published daily in the national press and are subject to fluctuations in interest rates generally.

Banks will also usually charge an arrangement fee on a bridging loan. This may be, for example, the greater of £100 or 50 pence per £100 of the amount of the loan.

There are several ways in which a bridging loan can be structured. Each calls for a progressively greater percentage of the overall borrowing to be acquired through bridging finance – the balance between being a long-term mortgage – and is therefore progressively more expensive.

As repayment of the bridging loan is made from the sale proceeds of the old home – a draw down of the new mortgage in some instances – the property must be readily saleable, mortgageable and realistically valued.

A seller with bridging finance remains in charge of the sale and so can place the old home on the market when and at what price he sees fit. As interest on the money borrowed is the major cost of bridging finance, it is essential that the borrower pitches his sale price at a level which ensures a quick sale but nonetheless permits him to take advantage of any upward price trend. As a rough guide: one percentage point on the price equals one month's interest.

People usually sell their old home for a few percentage points more than the professional valuation and, on average, open bridging loans are borrowed for between six and eight weeks. The manner in which the loan is structured combined with tax relief and the speed at which a sale can be achieved (based on realistic valuations) means that the total costs of bridging for most borrowers should not exceed about 2.5 per cent of the value of the old home. Add to this a further 3.5 per cent to cover the costs of selling – legal costs and estate agent's fees – and it is clear that bridging finance can be cheaper than the alternative, chainbreaking.

Moreover, most of these costs may well be recouped because, as with chainbreaking, the borrower has the ability to negotiate as a cash buyer.

CHAINBREAKING SERVICES

If the property buying chain comes to a complete standstill, you may find yourself unable to exchange contracts on your property in time to secure the property you are trying to buy. Here, a chainbreaking service may help. In appropriate cases they can intervene and buy your own property, breaking the chain and allowing you to complete your purchase.

Chainbreaking services are offered by major financial institutions and in some cases are only available to existing customers who are using, for example, the company's own estate agency services. There may be other stipulations, that the minimum market value of the property sold is £20,000, or that there is a genuine chain, i.e. the sale of at least two properties are interdependent.

THE COST

The offer will normally be between 88 and 92 per cent of the established market value. A chainbreaker must offer a price lower than your current selling price for two reasons. First, expenses are incurred in time spent, legal fees and the like. Second, the chainbreaker must sell the property again very quickly to avoid losing substantial interest on the capital outlay and to prevent it becoming an empty, depreciating asset.

Once the property is accepted under the scheme all selling costs including the interest on capital outlay are usually taken on by the chainbreaker, leaving you free to purchase your new home.

HOW TO APPLY

Your estate agent will advise you whether your property can be considered under the scheme and obtain an application form. This is accompanied by a request for a non-returnable fee of about £200 to cover initial administration and valuation costs.

On receiving your completed application form and the fee, the service will arrange two open market valuations of your property. The offer made will be based upon an average of these valuations, unless the difference between them exceeds 5 per cent. In this case a third valuation may be requested and the average of the two closest will be used. (The service does reserve the right, based on the valuations, not to make an offer on your property.) You will have seven days in which to accept or reject the offer. If you accept, you will normally have no estate agent's fee on the sale of your property.

RESALE AND COSTS

On receiving your acceptance, the chainbreaker will arrange for your property to be purchased as quickly as possible, leaving you free to complete your own purchase. This normally happens within 21 days of acceptance of the offer. Your solicitor will be contacted in order to carry out the necessary conveyancing.

The chainbreaker will decide the asking price for the property and arrange its resale. It will, of course, be necessary to have your co-operation in providing access to prospective buyers of the property.

Besides the non-returnable fee on application, there is the cost of conveyancing undertaken by your solicitor. The cost of the valuation of your property and the estate agent's fees for the sale of the property are included in the offer price.

PART II

LOANS

TYPES OF LOAN

Although a mortgage is the most common type of loan –
many people live with one for most of their working lives –
there are many others.

The difference between a mortgage and other types of
loan is that the mortgage is a secured loan. The lender
takes no real risk because he can always get his money
back by forcing you to sell your property. Most other loans
are unsecured. The lender takes the risk that you may run
away or be declared bankrupt, when he would have little
chance of recovering his money. That is why unsecured
loans are more expensive than mortgages. The higher
interest rate reflects the higher risk.

For some people the very idea of borrowing is abhorrent.
'Neither a borrower nor a lender be', though many people
who believe that make an exception of a mortgage. Islamic
fundamentalists object to both borrowing and lending on
religious grounds: usury is condemned by the Koran as it was
by the medieval Christian Church. But for most people
borrowing can be financial good sense. It can be in your
interest to buy goods straight away on borrowed money
rather than save up and buy them later.

In times of inflation, borrowing makes doubly good
sense. What you save by buying at today's prices can easily
cover the interest you pay on a loan. And the buying power
of what you pay in interest in repaying the loan decreases as
time passes and its value is eroded by inflation.

For example, if you borrow £100 and agree to pay the
£100 back at the end of the year together with £10 interest,
then at the end of the year you pay back £110. But suppose
inflation runs at 10 per cent over the year. Then the buying
power of the £110 you pay back is only £100. In real terms
the loan has cost you nothing. The way to work out the real

cost of borrowing is to subtract the rate of inflation from the APR (Annual Percentage Rate).

If you opted to save up for what you wanted to buy, you would earn interest on your money, but the savings you make by buying the goods at the beginning of the period could be more than the interest you earn.

HOW MUCH DO YOU HAVE TO PAY?

It cannot be said for certain that you will benefit if you buy now, instead of saving to buy later when the same goods may be more expensive. Whether you will or not depends on what you have to pay in interest and other charges for the money you borrow.

The cost of loans from various sources varies widely. Forms of credit like hire purchase, for example, can work out two or three times as costly as a bank overdraft.

It is easy to compare the cost of borrowing. Lenders are obliged to quote the APR on all their loans, which makes all borrowing directly comparable.

DIFFERENT TYPES OF LOAN

Loans differ from each other in more ways than their cost in terms of interest. Some are relatively long-term – up to five or ten years – others are short – a few weeks or months. Some have to be paid off in measured instalments, others more or less whenever the debtor feels like it. His credit rating will have a marked effect on loans from some sources, but mean little to others.

Some types of loans are inextricably tied to the goods you are buying, and no one would consider them otherwise. A hire-purchase (HP) loan is a good example. Other loans provide cash in hand and the money can be spent on anything. Overdrafts and insurance policy loans tend to be of this type – they generally have no conditions tied to them.

FLEXIBLE AND INFLEXIBLE LOANS

Between these two extremes of complete flexibility and complete inflexibility, there is a wide range of loans to choose from.

The fact that you borrow cash doesn't necessarily mean that the loan is entirely flexible. With an ordinary loan from the bank, for example, even though you get cash in hand, the bank manager will probably want to know what you intend to use the money for. If it's a personal loan, he certainly will.

Credit cards and store credit, although linked to the purchase of goods, are not inflexible in the way that HP or credit sale agreements are. If you buy goods with them that you would ordinarily pay cash for, they can be just as flexible as borrowing money. And with credit cards you can even get a direct cash advance though it is cheaper to conserve cash and spend as much as possible on the credit card, as you start paying interest on the cash advance from day one, whereas on goods you only pay interest on the balance outstanding after the next statement.

Often it is cheaper to borrow cash from your bank than to take out HP or other goods-related loans.

THE LENGTH OF THE LOAN

Before taking out a loan it is wise to look at your overall financial position, drawing up a detailed account of your incomings and outgoings if necessary. Decide how long a period you need to make the repayments, remembering that the longer the period of the loan, the lower the instalments. If you need the money for a very short time – two weeks perhaps – a credit card should tide you over. Provided you pay off the debt within 25 days of receiving the statement from the credit card company – which may not reach you for nearly a month from the date of the actual purchase, the loan won't cost you a penny.

As well as the length of loan, consider the timing of your repayments. How will it fit in with your overall budget? If your income is irregular as it is for many self-employed people, it may be more convenient to repay capital and interest in one lump sum at the end of the period rather than in regular instalments every month – the arrangement which usually suits someone with a regular salary.

If the loan is going to last more than a year, you should consider whether you would be able to manage in the event of illness, redundancy or some other unforeseen setback. Perhaps the lender will arrange insurance to cover the repayments.

Where your overall budget is concerned, the spacing of repayments and the time they continue can matter almost as much as their size.

YOUR FINANCIAL STANDING

No one will give you a loan in the first place unless they are reasonably sure of getting their money back. A lender will want to consider your past financial record, your current income and what security you can offer on the loan.

Someone with a poor credit record is obviously at a disadvantage. If, for example, you have had a court order made against you for debt and did not pay it off promptly, you will probably be on the files of a credit reference agency. Lenders check with these agencies. And if you are on their files, you may find it difficult to get the loan you want.

Lenders are also likely to ask for the name and address of your employer, bank manager, building society manager, landlord, etc. They may ask any of these for references, and may inform them of the size of your requested loans.

The lender will also almost certainly require details of your income along with details of regular financial commitments such as – your mortgage, rates, HP contracts, alimony, child-support payments and so on.

Obviously it is easier to obtain a loan – or to obtain one at more favourable rates – if satisfactory security is offered. This means offering the lender rights to assets which can be sold if the loan is not repaid. When the loan has been paid off, the rights naturally return to the borrower.

Apart from the rights to some of the capital invested in your house, which is the security for a mortgage, you can secure a loan with an insurance policy that has a cash-in value preferably higher than the value of the loan. Or you can offer rights to investments you may have such as stocks, shares, bonds, National Savings certificates, etc.

If you do not have such assets yourself, you may be able to obtain credit with a guarantee from a friend or a relative. Such an agreement should not be entered into lightly: if you default, your friend has to pay.

METHODS OF BORROWING

The best method of borrowing money depends on individual circumstances – How much do you need? How long do you need it for? What do you want to buy with the money? And so on. No single solution suits everyone. But whatever your situation, you should consider several alternatives.

Employers will sometimes provide a loan inexpensively or interest free. Some employers do this, for example, to help employees pay for season tickets. Some provide loans for a house or a car. There are other sources of preferential finance in trade unions and professional associations.

It may be possible to pay frequent bills by instalments. For example, the company that supplies oil for your central heating may agree to accept regular payments rather than one lump sum. However, you might be better off paying a regular amount into a savings account and withdrawing the money to pay the bills rather than paying the supplier in instalments.

If you want to borrow a large sum, perhaps £1,000 or more, and you are unable to get a cheap loan as suggested above, the first alternative is an insurance policy loan (or an increased mortgage if the loan is for home improvements). If that is impossible, an ordinary bank loan or personal bank loan should be obtained. If that fails, it is time to consider a finance-company loan, a second mortgage or HP.

For a smaller sum, with repayments spread over several years, the sequence is roughly the same, starting with an insurance policy loan. A second mortgage is obviously not suitable for a smaller loan.

If you intend to repay the loan fairly fast, try a credit card, a bank overdraft or other type of bank loan, then HP, an option account or mail order.

Whatever type of loan you require, don't take the first offer. Investigate the alternatives.

CREDIT CARDS

In the 1960s when credit cards first became part of everyday life, the arrival of the cashless society was widely predicted. It hasn't happened yet and some people have run into trouble with 'plastic money', building up debts they can't pay off. But for most of us, the plastic card has become a very useful means of instant credit.

There are 1,200 or more different types of credit card in circulation, counting those issued by individual stores. The most popular are general credit cards which allow repayment over an extended period, with interest charged on the amount outstanding. Some store cards charge almost 35 per cent a year while the two most widespread cards in Britain, Access and Visa, which are available through banks, currently charge 1.75 per cent a month or 23.1 per cent a year – a rate, incidentally, which compares unfavourably with the banks' own overdraft rates.

CHARGE CARDS
The well-known charge or travel and entertainment cards such as American Express and Diners Club offer insignificant advantages for most UK citizens. Holders of these cards pay an annual fee of about £40 and must pay off the full amount owing at the end of each month, conditions that do not apply to Access and Visa.

At present, there are 22 million Access and Visa card accounts in Britain against one million American Express and Diners Club accounts.

STORE AND TOWN CARDS
In-store cards are usually issued free and are sometimes linked to banks or building societies. There are three types, as defined by method of repayment. 'Budget' cards demand

regular monthly payments; others permit variable payments at the cardholder's discretion, and a third type requires settlement in full each month.

The interest payments on store card accounts are offset in many people's eyes by their convenience. As well as providing an instant source of purchasing power, they allow a period of up to six weeks between buying an article and paying for it. Cards are used mostly for petrol and motoring costs, clothing and footwear, travel and electrical goods. Interest rates on store cards are high, although several stores claim to be losing money on their card schemes.

In the wake of store cards came a more ambitious idea which has so far proved very successful – town cards. Three towns – Chester, Wilmslow and Tunbridge Wells – operate a credit card scheme which is available to residents, the cards being accepted by local traders. The concept was devised by Paul Robinson, a member of Wilmslow's chamber of commerce, and organised by a Liverpool financial company, Credit and Data Marketing Services. The Wilmslow scheme went into operation in September 1985, Tunbridge Wells and Chester followed early in 1986. Several other towns are currently discussing their own schemes with CDMS.

ADVANTAGES

One advantage of using credit cards is the protection given under the Consumer Credit Act. If a supplier of goods or services does not provide either satisfactorily, both the supplier and the credit-card company are liable. For example, when Laker Airways went bankrupt, customers who had paid for tickets by credit card got their money back – those who had paid by other methods did not.

Compensation can be claimed from either the supplier or the credit card company for anything costing between £100 and £30,000. But charge cards – even gold charge cards (see below) – are not covered.

Credit cards can be expensive if you fail to keep vigilant watch on expenditure. However, there are ways to limit the cost of your borrowing on credit cards. For example, it pays to have two credit cards, with settlement dates as widely separated as possible – one at the end of the month, say, and the other in the middle. Use the card with the most interest-free credit weeks left. Note also that there are two dates on your statement, the billing date and the payment-by date. Any transaction after the billing date will be carried forward to the next one – so you won't have to pay for those for a further two weeks.

You should endeavour to pay the balance each month. If you pay off the full amount you won't have to pay interest. The idea is to use the card as an alternative to paying cash – not as a means of credit. It is important to keep your receipts, so you can check them against your monthly statement. The system is not infallible. Mistakes can be made. Be careful not to leave receipt carbons lying about. Criminals have learned that the carbon copies thrown away at restaurants and stores reveal people's credit-card numbers, which they can use to buy goods and services by phone. Ask for the carbons back and destroy them.

Cash borrowed on a card doesn't benefit from the interest-free period up to the first settlement date. You start paying interest from the date of the advance and it is therefore unprofitable to use a credit card for a cash advance. If possible, use alternatives such as a cash-dispenser card or cheque guarantee card.

All credit-card holders are limited by the company to a certain maximum sum. If you need to buy something that would break your credit limit, a telephone call to the credit card company will usually secure a concession.

NEW DEVELOPMENTS
Changes in the law now allow building societies and other financial institutions to perform what used to be exclusively

banking services. The issue of credit cards is an example. The first financial institution to enter this market was Save & Prosper, which launched the Classic credit card in 1987. Although issued under the Visa umbrella, it marked a new step in the credit card business.

The main difference between Classic and other credit cards is the interest charged on the proportion of your bill, if any, that is unpaid at the end of the month. Classic currently charges 1.5 per cent a month, which is an APR of 19.6 per cent. Most high street banks currently charge 1.75 per cent a month – some charge 1.9 per cent – and certain store cards, such as those issued by Boots and Sears, charge up to 2.5 per cent (APR 34.4 per cent).

While undercutting on interest rates, Save & Prosper have compensated to some extent by restricting their card to people who are likely to be good credit risks. To qualify you must be a home-owner in salaried employment who has not moved home or changed jobs in the previous 12 months. Salaried status must be proved by producing a P60 form for the previous year or the most recent salary slip. A mortgage statement or solicitor's letter are required as proof of home ownership.

There are two other innovative features. First, the cardholder can choose the time of the month when his credit card bill must be paid before interest charges begin. If his salary is paid on the first of the month, he can arrange for the credit card bill to be settled shortly afterwards.

The second new feature is an option to pay the bill by direct debit at the end of the interest-free period. This ensures the full benefit from the interest-free period, and abolishes the need to write a monthly cheque and post it.

One unsatisfactory feature of the the high street banks' credit cards is that it is really quite difficult to extract the full benefit of interest-free credit. If you send your cheque when you receive your bill, the bank will cash it immediately although you do not have to pay for another twenty days or so.

Nor does postdating the cheque deter them. But if you wait until the last moment before paying, you risk missing the deadline, in which case you have to pay with interest charges from the day the bill was sent.

However, there is also a disadvantage in taking the direct-debit option on the Classic card: you have to settle your bill in full every month, which may sometimes prove to be inconvenient. The card also costs £3 a year.

DEBT

It is easy to forget how much you are spending when you use plastic money and a growing problem today is the level of credit card debt. The Bank of England's quarterly economic reports show a sharp increase in the number of households facing severe debt problems and note that the average age of debtors is falling. Organisations ranging from the Office of Fair Trading to the Association of County Councils and the Money Advice Association are beginning to question the methods of many banks and stores which urge people to buy more than they can afford and to that end provide them with almost unlimited credit.

Citizens' Advice Bureaux handle over 500,000 cases of chronic debt a year. Those debts amount to over £500 million and 6 per cent of that is due to overload on credit cards.

GOLD CARDS

Credit card companies offer gold cards to high income earners. These cards carry guaranteed overdrafts of up to £10,000 and above with lower-than-normal APR. They are quick to arrange, convenient and available for any purpose. No security is required and repayments are flexible.

However, besides being limited to the high-income bracket, tax relief cannot be claimed on the interest (unless the expenditure is for business purposes), and there is a subscription of about £40 a year.

STORE CREDIT

Most large stores and shops are eager to offer credit because, they believe, it encourages people to buy from them.

SHOP BUDGET ACCOUNT

Some stores run save-and-borrow or shop budget accounts. The customer has to pay into the account a certain monthly sum, and in return the store will lend the customer something like 25 or 30 times as much. These accounts are an attractive way of borrowing because they can be arranged on the spot. For a small payment you can walk away with a lot of goods.

On the other hand, the rate of interest is often high. Payments into the account are usually made by direct debit or standing order, and it is all too easy to go on paying into the account long after the goods have been paid for. You do sometimes receive interest when the account is in credit, but it is usually less than you would get if you invested the money elsewhere, though more than it would earn in a current account at the bank, on which no interest is paid.

SHOP OPTION ACCOUNT

Shops now issue their own credit cards. You can only use them in that store or another branch, but otherwise the card works exactly like a Visa or Access card, though you cannot get a cash advance. The APR is about the same as Visa and Access too, which is more than you may be able to borrow from another source. These cards are convenient, however, especially to someone frequently patronising the same store.

HIRE PURCHASE

Hire purchase, conditional sale and credit sale are all tied to the purchase of particular goods and work rather like personal loans. They are paid off in instalments at a fixed interest rate.

Under HP and conditional sale agreements, the goods don't belong to you until you have paid off the whole amount borrowed. Until then you are hiring them and if repayment fails the store can repossess them. On a credit sale the goods belong to you straight away. This can be an expensive way to borrow but, as with a credit account, the convenience alone is worth something.

The term hire purchase is often used to cover three different types of credit, all normally arranged by the vendor. These are real hire purchase, credit sale and conditional sale. Finance company personal loans may also be thought of as HP as they are often offered with specific purposes in mind, such as buying a car. But there are importance differences between the three types.

With HP agreements, you are technically hiring the goods either from the retailer or from the finance company, which has technically bought them from the retailer. You cannot therefore resell the goods until you have made the last payment.

Hire purchase is controlled by government regulations which specify that you must pay a deposit on certain goods. You normally pay in monthly instalments for a period of three years or less. Security is not required as the goods do not yet belong to you. The retailer or the finance company can repossess them. But once you have paid one-third of the value of the goods (including your deposit), they can only do so with a court order (so long as the HP price is £5,000 or less).

The cost varies widely from nothing to an APR of over 60 per cent. With free credit, however, you may be unable to take advantage of substantial discounts.

As you are technically hiring the goods, you have the right to end the agreement and return the goods but you will have to pay any overdue instalments and you may have to pay half the total price if your payments have not reached that point. If the goods have been damaged during your possession of them, you will have to pay compensation to the lender.

If the shop or finance company points out any defects in the goods which are noted in the HP agreement, you can't return them and the lender can disclaim responsibility for the defects. The same applies if the goods are stated as being second-hand.

It is often cheaper to borrow the money and pay cash than to buy on HP, but not so convenient.

CREDIT SALE

Credit sale may seem much like HP, because the shop normally arranges for you pay by instalments. But the goods are yours from the start; you can't send them back if you change your mind and the lender can't repossess them if you fail to keep up the payments. The agreement may include a clause requiring you, if you sell the goods before you have paid in full, to pay the balance owing at once, but early re-payment normally results in some reduction in the interest charged.

CONDITIONAL SALE

In a conditional sale, the vendor owns the goods until the purchaser has fulfilled certain conditions, including completion of payments. Apart from the fact that you are not technically hiring the goods – the vendor is letting you use them while you pay – the terms are much same as for hire purchase.

DEPOSIT REGULATIONS

The government lays down rules controlling the period of credit and the size of the deposit in the purchase of certain articles on HP or credit sale. Other lenders, like banks and finance companies, normally apply similar limits to loans. For example, on loans to buy domestic equipment (washing machines, freezers, hi-fi equipment, cameras, watches, jewellery, etc.), the minimum deposit is one-fifth of the cash price and the maximum period of the loan is two-and-a-half years.

These limits also apply to loans for television sets, but for teletext receivers the minimum deposit is one-tenth of the cash price (the maximum length of the loan is the same). If buying a car for private use, the minimum deposit is 20 per cent of the cash price and the maximum period is three years; for business use, depending on creditworthiness, up to four years with a deposit as little as 10 per cent.

HP OR CASH?

Customers may be offered a discount for paying cash. But sometimes HP prices can be cheaper because the vendor receives a commission from the finance company. Arguments over which is the better deal are particularly common in the case of cars, when a position is often complicated by part-exchange of an old vehicle. Free or inexpensive HP terms are offered by some garages and department stores and most mail-order companies.

If you have a choice between buying on HP and paying cash with money borrowed elsewhere, you will have some difficult sums to do. First, ascertain the lowest cash price, taking account of any discount, then subtract the amount of the HP deposit. Do you have enough cash to pay for the item?

If you do, what interest could you earn if you invested this amount – in a building society for instance – and withdrew enough each month to pay the instalments.

Add this interest to the cheapest cash price, and you have the effective cost of paying cash. If it is less than the HP price (the total of all the HP payments including the deposit), it is probably cheaper to pay cash. If not, take the HP.

Suppose you don't have enough cash to pay for the item and must therefore borrow. What would the monthly payments be if you borrowed the amount from, for example, a bank and repaid it in the same period as the HP agreement? If the loan repayments total less than the HP instalments, borrow the money and pay cash. If not, take the HP.

A man plans to buy a car for £3,600 and is offered a discount of £300 if he pays cash. Alternatively, he can take a 24-month HP agreement at low cost through the dealer. Agreements vary between dealers. In one such case, the man must pay a deposit of one-third of the price – £1,200 – and monthly instalments of £115, making the total HP price £3,960. The cheapest cash price is £3,300. After subtracting the amount of the deposit – £1,200 – the amount left to pay is £2,100.

If he is able to pay cash for the car and invests that amount in a building society at 8.5 per cent, over two years he earns £178.50. So the effective cost of paying cash is £3,300 + £178.50, or £3,478.50. That is less than the total HP price, and is therefore the better option.

If he has insufficient cash, he can borrow the money from his bank. A personal loan of £2,100 over 24 months involves him in monthly instalments of about £104. This is less than the monthly HP instalments of £115, and is again preferable to the HP scheme.

FINANCE COMPANIES

These companies provide most of the finance for shop credit schemes, and they also offer other types of loan. Approaching a finance company direct can be productive if you have difficulty raising a loan elsewhere. You don't have to be a customer already, as you do with many bank loans. The arrangements are usually speedy and simple, and you may be able to borrow a larger sum than a bank would countenance.

A finance company loan arranged by a shop or other trader has another advantage. If the goods you buy later prove faulty, you may have a claim against the finance company as the lender as well as the vendor (if the value of the goods is over £100).

The cost of these loans varies dramatically. Some companies offer very competitive rates, others charge considerably more than banks or other lenders.

INTEREST-FREE CREDIT

If we borrow money, we expect to pay interest. But there are ways to avoid it.

STORE CREDIT

Many stores offer interest-free credit as a sales incentive. By law, this must be genuinely interest free; it should not be possible to buy the same goods at the same store for a lower price by paying cash.

Usually, no security is required and there are no penalties if you pay off the loan early. Otherwise, you will have to go through the regular assessment of your income and commitments and undergo a credit check.

Obviously interest-free store credit is beneficial to the customer. There is just one point to bear in mind: Can you buy the same goods cheaper in another store?

EMPLOYER'S LOANS

Large employers often offer loans interest-free or at a very low interest rate to assist employees purchasing – typically – homes, cars and season tickets. It is prudent to find out what would happen if you leave the company or if it closes down. You may also be liable for income tax on this 'perk'.

CREDIT CARDS

If you use your credit card wisely you can take advantage of up to eight weeks of free credit. When you buy goods with a credit card you pay nothing until your next statement arrives and the first payment is due. As the statements are submitted monthly, you have about four weeks to pay. So, if you buy goods on a credit card at the beginning of a statement period, you will have to pay no interest for that period plus the four weeks or so allowed for payment. Credit card companies receive a discount on the price of their clients' purchases, so they are still making money even if they receive no interest.

Admittedly, only a highly organised person can take full advantage of this system, buying at the beginning of the statement period and paying off the entire amount by the payment date. And the most difficult part of the operation is to exploit the maximum interest-free period without overrunning the deadline, which means paying interest for the whole of the following month.

Interest-free borrowing on credit cards is only possible when you are buying goods. If you borrow cash on your credit card, you are charged interest immediately.

CHARGE CARDS

Charge cards like American Express and Diners Club can be regarded as a type of interest-free credit. No interest is payable on the amount advanced to pay the relevant bill, but the entire debt must be paid off at the end of the month, and it is not really free because although you pay no interest, you do have to pay an enrolment fee to acquire the card as well as subsequent annual fees to retain it.

BANK LOANS

Banks are in business to lend money. Most people have bank accounts and the bank manager is often the first person to turn to when extra money is needed. There are a number of different ways of borrowing from a bank, some cheaper or more flexible than others, and the wisest borrower will consider the various options before applying for a loan.

OVERDRAFTS

Most people discover overdrafts in the worst possible way. They find from their bank statements that they have spent more money than they earned before the end of the month, and their accounts have plunged into the red.

If you are going to have an overdraft it is best to ask your bank manager first. He is unlikely to refuse as the bank charges a relatively high rate of interest on an overdraft. But he may discuss with you your financial situation and set some limit on your borrowing. You can get some useful financial advice this way.

Bank overdrafts are convenient and quick to arrange. You can use the money for any purpose and security is not usually required. But you can't get tax relief on your interest payments, unless your spending is for business purposes, and the interest rate is somewhat deceptive.

When you overdraw you naturally incur charges for falling below the free-banking limit. This raises the effective APR considerably. The bank can also insist that you pay off your overdraft at any time and it may charge you an arrangement fee at the outset.

APRs currently vary from 16.4 per cent to 23.9 per cent if the overdraft is authorised by your bank manager – but it is effectively much higher if you are currently enjoying free banking.

ORDINARY LOANS

When you take out an ordinary bank loan, the bank places the money in your current account, which should therefore remain in credit and, with luck, above the free-banking limit. The bank opens a separate loan account into which you make your regular payments.

This is cheaper than a personal loan from the bank (see below) and as each loan is usually negotiated individually, it can be tailored to suit your particular needs. This makes it a good form of medium-term borrowing – up to about ten years. Arrangement fees may be payable.

Ordinary loans are not available to every customer and the bank may encourage you to get a personal loan instead.

PERSONAL LOANS

A bank's personal loan is an 'off-the-shelf' loan and is available for most purposes. It is normally obtained quickly and easily and no security is needed. It is not necessary to be a customer of that bank, although you may be asked to open an account. Building societies now also offer personal loans.

Personal loans tend to be a rather expensive form of borrowing and they are also comparatively inflexible. You may be charged a penalty if you repay the loan early. The maximum term is usually five to seven years and the maximum loan is about £7,500, or less. The APR is currently around 21 per cent and may be as much as 24 per cent, and the rate is fixed when you take out the loan.

HOME IMPROVEMENT LOANS

Some banks offer special home improvement loans. They are usually cheaper than personal loans. The maximum limit is higher and the term may be up to ten years.

But, of course, you have to spend the money you borrow on home improvements, and security is often required. You may not be able to borrow all of the costs of any home improvement. And you may be charged a penalty if you repay the loan early. The typical current APR is between 16.7 and 23.9 per cent. The interest may qualify for tax relief.

BUDGET ACCOUNTS

If you find budgeting for regular expenditure difficult, a budget account can help – at a cost. What you have to do is to add up your expected outgoings for the year – your household bills essentially – and divide the total by twelve. You deposit that sum in the budget account every month and use it to pay your bills. Sometimes these are more than the account is holding: so a budget account is simply a current account with a built-in overdraft facility.

The drawback is that the interest payable when the account is overdrawn is higher than that on an ordinary overdraft, and not all accounts give you interest when you are in credit. There may be other bank charges too.

INSURANCE POLICY AND PENSION LOANS

Borrowing money is always cheaper and simpler if you can offer the lender some form of security – especially if you are borrowing more than £5,000. The savings you build up in an insurance policy or a pension are one form of security you can offer.

INSURANCE POLICY LOANS

Loans secured against the surrender value of a life insurance policy are often cheap, and it is only necessary to repay the interest during the life of the loan. You can leave the loan outstanding until the policy pays out or repay earlier if you prefer. You also get the continued benefit of your life policy and this method is therefore, in most circumstances a much better way of raising cash than surrendering the policy.

However, if the policy has been running for only a short time, the amount you can borrow is likely to be very small: the maximum loan is a percentage of the policy's surrender value. These loans are not available with all life policies and you can't raise a loan in this way if the policy is already employed for another purpose such as repaying your mortgage. Another disadvantage is that, along with the interest on the loan, you have to continue to pay the policy premiums.

PENSION LOANS

As well as using a pension plan to get a mortgage, companies can also borrow money against their pension plans. The plans must be for controlling directors i.e. the directors must own or control more than 5 per cent of the company. And the lender may require detailed information on the purpose of the loan.

The loan can be up to 50 per cent of the money accumulated in the pension fund, provided this does not exceed the amount which would be available were a director to retire early. The initial loan is usually set at about £5,000, and further loans of £2,000 or more can be taken as reserves increase, but there must be regular contributions to the pension plan, usually of at least £2,500 a year. The term of the loan runs until one year before the retirement date in the pension plan.

The lender does not usually require details of the borrower's financial status or ability to repay, but may in certain circumstances reserve the right to refuse the loan. No collateral security is required, as the lender puts a legal charge on the pension plan.

The interest rate which normally applies to this sort of loan is about 3 per cent above the clearing banks' base rate, though there is a lag when rates change. And the interest is usually payable every six months.

The loan has to be repaid immediately if a director dies, changes companies or retires early, and on termination of the pension plan or non-payment of interest.

If the repayment of the loan is not made when due, the lender would take all other reasonable steps to obtain repayments before applying to the policy for his security. Repaying the loan in this way inevitably reduces the retirement benefits. The first to suffer is the tax-free cash sum. Remaining benefits will be restricted to those which can be provided by the remaining part of the fund.

It is possible to repay the loan in full at any time, though notice of about six months' is usually required. It must not be repaid later than twelve months before the director's normal retiring date specified under the pension plan. Partial repayment can normally be made at any time – again usually subject to six months notice – though repayments are often restricted to amounts of more than £1,000 on amounts outstanding which exceed £3,000.

CREDIT RATING

Whether you like it or not, you have a credit rating. Wherever your financial details are kept, your rating will have been worked out and there is precious little you can do about it.

CREDIT SCORING

The best-known statistical system for working out an individual's credit rating is called credit scoring. Certain financial and non-financial characteristics of the applicant are evaluated according to a formula, usually in table form. The table is derived from the creditor's past experience with similar applicants and allocates points to each of the selected characteristics according to the applicant's responses. If the total points fail to reach a predetermined cut-off point, the applicant is rejected. If the score falls in a grey area around the pass mark, lenders may exercise their judgement, one way or another. This method of assessing a person's credit-worthiness is being used by an increasing number of lenders.

A voluntary code of practice called *A Guide to Credit Scoring*, which lays down guidelines for fair and objective systems, has been drawn up by several groups in the credit business in consultation with the Office of Fair Trading. Under this code the lender is obliged to inform the applicant if credit scoring is being used and, if he or she is rejected, to explain why. However, not all lenders subscribe to this code.

After pioneering work in the United States, the use of credit-scoring systems has grown significantly in the UK, largely due to the recent economic recession and associated growth of bad debt.

It is unfortunate that credit rating is surrounded by secrecy. You can never be sure how you score. But there are obvious facts which credit-rating agencies take into consideration. First, income. If you make a lot of money that's good. If you make a lot of money regularly that's even better. Agencies are impressed by a high income but prefer it to derive from a salary.

Steady employment is another asset. A steady sort with a steady income who does not go job hopping is a better risk. Owning your own home helps too. It means that you have – or soon will have – some equity behind you. If you have a mortgage, someone must have already regarded you as a fit person to borrow money.

Comparative youth is advantageous – not so young as to be irresponsible but young enough to have many earning years ahead. The married state is regarded favourably – there may be a second income to act as a financial safety net – but children are a mixed blessing. They contribute towards a stable existence but they are an extra expense.

Insurance policies help, and good health is very important. You are not going to be able to pay back the loan if you are seriously ill – or dead.

On the debit side, earlier financial problems, if known, can be a black mark against you. If a judgement has been made against you in a County Court, that fact will be recorded, and unless settlement was then made promptly, a County Court judgement would have been registered against you. If you settle later, it will cost you £1 to wipe clean your record – but it won't be expunged from the record for five to seven years.

CREDIT AGENCIES

These collect information about your financial standing and keep records of unpaid court judgements and the like. Many lenders refer to these agencies before offering a loan. You have a right to check any information they hold which relates to you.

Any lender with whom you negotiate for a loan must inform you of the name and address of any agency used, providing you request the information within 28 days of finishing loan negotiations. You can write to the agency enclosing a fee of £1 and ask for a copy of your file. If it contains false information you can ask for it to be removed. Within 28 days of receiving your letter, the agency must inform you whether or not it has fulfilled your request, and if you are not satisfied with the response you can write your own correction of up to 200 words and insist that it is attached to your file.

The Data Protection Act has strengthened and expanded the citizen's rights where financial records are kept on computer. It gives individuals the right to examine personal records held on computer not only by credit-reference agencies but also by banks, finance houses, credit-card companies and even department stores and mail-order companies, but tracking down the source of spurious data can still be extremely difficult owing to the sheer complexity of the financial network. Most financial institutions, and even some banks, freely swap personal financial files to build up even larger dossiers, and discovering the original source of the false story may be an impossible job.

THE SAFEGUARDS

Borrowers often think of themselves as helpless in the hands of large financial institutions, especially if they have got themselves into trouble over debt. In fact they are far from helpless. The law gives a great deal of support to the individual and every borrower should know their rights.

THE TRUE RATE OF INTEREST

The law states that lenders must tell the borrower the 'total charge for credit' expressed as an interest rate – that is, the Annual Percentage Rate (APR). All quotations and detailed advertisements for credit (excluding prestige advertisements that merely mention the name of the bank along with lush film of, for example, a galloping horse) have to quote the APR. A written quotation must be provided for loans over £50 for goods and services if requested. In the case of a loan from a store, more detailed regulations specify the information that must be provided, including the frequency of payments, the amount of the instalments, the total amount to be paid, the cash price and of course the APR. The regulations are laid down in the 1974 Consumer Credit Act and only apply to loans up to £15,000, but mortgages above that figure are also covered.

LICENCING

Anyone who provides, arranges or advises on loans has to be licensed by the Office of Fair Trading. It is not only the lender who must be licenced. Shops which offer store cards or arrange hire purchase must be licenced, and so must credit brokers, debt collectors and any person who advises on credit. Local authorities and public bodies like the gas and electricity boards are exempt.

Licenses apart, the doorstep selling of credit is illegal, unless a visit from a company offering credit has been requested or the credit is arranged by someone selling the goods subject to the loan on the doorstep.

Credit brokers cannot charge you more than £3 for their services if the loan which they have arranged is not taken up within six months of their finding a lender.

COOLING-OFF PERIOD

You may have the right to a cooling-off period in which you may change your mind about a loan. You can cancel credit agreements between £50 and £15,000 if you have discussed the credit deal face-to-face with the lender and signed the agreement at home – or anywhere other than the lender's business premises.

When you sign a credit agreement you should get a copy of it. Every copy of the agreement should have a section which points out your right to cancel, and outlines the provision for a cooling-off period if applicable. After about a week another copy – or a separate notice of your cancellation rights – should be mailed to you. From the day after you receive this, you have a further five days in which you may cancel.

Even if you have taken out a cash loan, you can cancel the agreement without charge provided you repay the loan within one month or before the first payment is due. This applies where the loan is unsecured, or secured other than with a land mortgage. Where land mortgages are used as security the above provisions will apply with minor modifications.

FAULTY GOODS

If goods bought with a loan prove faulty, you can claim against the lender as well as the retailer. For example, if you bought central heating from a company which also arranged a loan for you, you could claim from the lender as well as the central heating company if your boiler blows up.

However, this safeguard only applies if the full cash price of the goods or services is between £100 and £30,000; if the amount of the loan is below £15,001 (regardless of whether it covers the full cost), and if credit was offered under a standing arrangement between the supplier of the goods and the lender. With HP agreements, your legal rights are against the finance company alone.

EARLY REPAYMENT PENALTIES

Where for any reason a loan is settled early the lender may impose extra charges to cover their administration charges or lost interest, or a combination of both. Normally this ranges from a £5 administration fee to a charge of three months' interest (often referred to as an 'interest adjustment'), but it may be more. However, not all lenders make a charge.

It is legal for a lender to charge compensation for lost interest if you make early repayment of a credit agreement which was scheduled for a set period. But the law does acknowledge that such a charge is unfair if you have to pay all the interest and charges for which you would have been liable if the loan had run its full term. So the amount you have to pay in most cases is reduced by a rebate worked out in accordance with certain regulations laid down by law. Again, these regulations apply only to loans between £50 and £15,000. If you contemplate the possibility of re-paying early, find a lender who won't impose a penalty.

If you want to end an HP agreement before term by returning the goods, you must pay at least half the total amount payable.

IF YOU'RE IN THE WRONG

If you fail to keep your part of the credit agreement, you still have some rights. The lender must give at least seven days' notice before calling in any loan early. If the loan was part of an HP agreement and you have already paid at least one-third of the total price, the finance company cannot repossess the goods without your permission or without a court order.

THE COST OF BORROWING

The annual percentage rate of charge – or APR – is the standard way of calculating the cost of borrowing, and the government requires that all lenders quote it so that borrowers are not misled by weekly, monthly and annual rates with varying fees which cannot easily be compared. APR permits a straightforward comparison: the higher the APR, the more expensive the loan.

APR

When mortgagees lend you money, they too are obliged to quote the APR, which equates the current value of the repayments with the advance the borrower receives. With repayment mortgages, most building societies calculate interest payments using 'annual rests'. The amount of interest charged is based on the outstanding mortgage debt at the beginning of the year, regardless of the fact that some of the debt is repaid each month. But the banks – with the exception of National Westminster – calculate the interest on a monthly basis; their APRs are accordingly lower for the same nominal rates charged by the building societies.

The APR takes into account not only the interest but also any service charge such as arrangement or acceptance fees and also any payments you have to make for a compulsory maintenance contract or premiums for certain insurance policies. The extra cost incurred if you buy on credit from a shop which normally gives a cash discount is also included.

The APR takes into account how much you actually owe at different times during the loan. Any loan which is repaid in instalments naturally decreases with each payment. For example, if you borrow £200 at the beginning of a year and pay it off in twelve monthly instalments, you owe the full £200 for one month only. At the end of the month, your first instalment would reduce the amount of debt. At the end of the year the loan is repaid and the debt is zero; therefore, averaged over the whole year, the debt is half the original amount – that is, £100.

If the original loan is taken at an interest rate of 12 per cent, the payment over the year is 12 per cent of £200, or £24. But £24 interest on an average debt of £100 works out at an APR of 24 per cent.

Naturally, the situation is much more complicated with a mortgage. But the principle is the same. The APR allows you to compare precisely a repayment mortgage – where the amount of the loan does decrease over the year – with an interest-only mortgage such as an endowment or pension-linked mortgage, where the capital sum does not decrease.

INFLATION

Theoretically, to work out the rate of interest on a loan in real terms you should subtract the rate of inflation. If you are paying interest at 17 per cent and the rate of inflation is 7 per cent, the true interest rate is only 10 per cent. Of course, this is only valid if your earnings are keeping step with inflation.

IF YOU CAN'T PAY

Due to unemployment and other causes, many people find they are unable to repay mortgages and loans. In that situation, the borrower should contact the lender immediately. It is to their advantage to help, since if the borrower fails to repay the loan it is they who suffer. They may be prepared to rearrange payments to fit a reduced budget. If you have a repayment mortgage, your lender may allow you to pay the interest only, with no capital repayments for a period.

When people examine their spending they can usually find items which can be cut down. Make sure, too, that you are not paying too much tax and that you are getting all the tax relief for which you are eligible. Perhaps you are also eligible for state benefits of some kind. Do not surrender an investment-type life insurance policy if you can avoid it, as the surrender value will compare unfavourably with what you have paid in premiums. It may be wiser to make it a paid-up policy, i.e. ceasing payment of the premiums, or a policy loan may be available.

Do not be tempted to take out another loan to help pay off the first. You could find yourself paying interest on the interest. Your bank manager may be helpful. He has more experience of similar situations, and he may suggest ways of consolidating your debts in one loan. You can also find help, especially if you believe the lender is infringing the Consumer Credit Act, at a Citizens' Advice Bureau, Consumer Advice Centre or the Trading Standards or Consumer Protection Department of your local council. The Office of Fair Trading publishes a number of useful leaflets on borrowing.

INSURANCE PROTECTION

Many lenders offer insurance to pay off the loan if the borrower dies or becomes unable to work through accident, illness or sometimes redundancy. Insurance may even be automatically included.

If it would be difficult for your family to repay the loan, such insurance is only prudent. However, the insurance offered by the lender may not be the best available. The Consumers' Association recommends that you consider your insurance needs in detail and choose policies to cover each one. However, you might have to make an exception if you need redundancy insurance, which is not easily obtained separately.